With Winning In Mind

The Mental Management® System

An Olympic Champion's Success System

by

Lanny R. Bassham
World and Olympic Champion

Mental Management ® is owned by Lanny R. Bassham

Copyright © 1995 by Lanny Bassham
First Edition Copyright ©1988 by Lanny Bassham
All rights reserved
ISBN 1-885221-47-9
Library of Congress 96-84757

Printed in the United States of America

LANNY BASSHAM
www.mentalmanagement.com
1-800-879-5079

Dedication

To Helen, my reason for winning.

Acknowledgements

To the Son of Man through Whom all things are possible.

To the memory of William and Natalou Bassham for the fundamental values.

To my wife Helen, my sons Brian and Troy, and my daughter Heather for making me feel like a champion.

To Rich and Jay for the possible dream.

To all Olympians for the inspiration.

To the U.S. Army Marksmanship Unit for the opportunity.

To all my students, including the Olympic teams of Japan, Australia, Canada, Republic of China, and the United States of America for their confidence.

To Todd Woodard for helping me find the words.

To four-time Olympian, Lyle Nelson, for the final edit.

Journey Of A Dream

A dream is born in the mind,
A picture of what might be —
A vision of a new and better life.
But if it stays in the mind,
It becomes another wish unfulfilled.

It must move on

The dream moves to the heart,
Feelings surround it, giving it life.
But if it stays in the heart,
It becomes a "could have been,"
Dying in the fire of emotion.

It must move on.

The dream moves to the hands,
There to be put into action.
Having been given life in the heart,
It comes to fruition through work.
But if the dream stays in your hands,
It becomes self-serving.

It must move on.

So place your hand in the hand of another,
And the dream moves on ... forever.

– Lanny Bassham

Contents

Introduction

Most people do not read introductions because most introductions are just too darn long. So I will try to make this one short. In fact, I made this entire book short, to the point, and easy to read. It is my desire that you be able to read this book in one sitting and understand what the Mental Management System is all about.

Are you interested in winning or helping others to win? If so, then this book is written for you. I believe there exists a mental system that will speed up the process of getting to the winners circle. I have dedicated the last twenty years of my life to searching out, refining, and using this system.

I am well aware there are many self improvement books available. They are written by psychologists, motivational speakers, religious leaders and business professionals. This one is written by an Olympic champion. What I am and what I teach is

the result of winning and losing. I did my appren-
ticeship in the arena of Olympic competition. My
credibility is in my gold medals and the medals of
my students. I have the great honor of knowing,
competing with, teaching and coaching more
Olympians than anyone I know.

My goal in this book is to share the winning
techniques of Olympic champions with you. This
little book has literally changed the performances of
people around the world. I will approach the book as
if you and I were talking together. It is the only way
I know to teach and achieve results.

Section I

What Is Mental Management?

Chapter 1

It Doesn't Matter If You Win Or Lose — Until You Lose!

I wanted to be a winner! For as long as I can remember, I have loved winning. I noticed in elementary school that the kids who won the races were always the happiest. All the other kids would come up to them and say, "That was great, you're super!" But it never happened to me. I never won a race in my life. I wasn't even good enough to be average. You know what they say about average: the best of the worst or the worst of the best! Well, I was the worst of the worst.

No one ever comes up to the loser and says, "Nice job!" unless it is a rebuke. I was always smaller, slower, and weaker than the winners. I wanted the recognition, but I was unable to earn it as an individual. So, I decided to try out for team sports.

I was the last person picked on the baseball team. I got alternate right field. If you have ever played Little League baseball, you know that they seldom hit the ball to right field. So that's where you put your worst player. And I was the alternate.

I still remember one day very well. I was in right field, and I heard a funny crack of the bat. A ball had been hit to me. I had never seen a ball like that before. It was smoking and heading straight for me. I couldn't get out of the way. I had to catch it. I put up my glove, reached for the ball, and it hit me right between the eyes. Two runs scored before I could throw it in. The coach was more than a little upset with me.

I went home and told my father, "I'm no good!" He said, "No! You are mistaken. There is nothing wrong with you, son. You haven't found what you are good at yet. Keep looking. Why not try something where the balls are bigger and easier to catch?"

So the next year I tried out for basketball. The balls were bigger and easier to catch. The coach carefully selected the players and their positions. The guards, center, and forwards were selected. I remained on the bench. That's where I sat out the season. Again, I was the last one to play in the games, and I was beginning to develop a super-low self-image.

I especially remember one game. The ball got away from one of the other team's players and bounced toward me. This time I knew exactly what to do. I would take the ball in for an easy lay-up and be a hero for the first time in my life. As I got to the ball, a thought crossed my mind: Is that our goal or is the other one ours? I had forgotten. In my moment of indecision, I accidentally kicked the ball out of play. Again, the coach was not too impressed with me. I was a failure in everything I had tried, and I was ready to give up on sports.

People say that it doesn't matter if you win or lose. But when you lose, it matters a lot. It hurts! The only things that kept me from quitting were the books on the Olympics. I loved the Olympic Games. I wanted more than anything to see them in person. I wanted to meet an Olympic gold medalist just once. I thought that if I could stand near them, some of their power would rub off on me.

Then one day a friend of mine told me that he was going to the rifle range. I asked, "Rifle shooting, what is that?"

"It is an Olympic sport," he said. Shooting is an Olympic sport? I was interested.

"How strong do you have to be to be a rifle shooter?" I asked.

"You don't have to be strong!" he said.

"How tall do you have to be to be a rifle shooter?"

"You don't have to be tall!"

"How fast do you have to be to be a shooter?"

"You don't understand," he replied. "You don't have to be tall or strong or fast. All you have to do is stand still."

"Great!" I exclaimed. "An Olympic sport where all you have to do is be still. I can do that! I've had lots of practice in the dugout and on the bench." That was the beginning of my shooting career.

My father saw this might be a way for me to develop some self-confidence. He encouraged me. He bought me the best equipment. He took up the sport as well. We practiced together, went to matches together and became a team. You see, Dad never played baseball or football either. My father and I became best friends on the rifle range.

I don't remember much about growing up. I was too busy training. When all the other kids went to movies, I practiced. I trained an average of five hours a day, five days a week for ten years before I made my first Olympic team. I shot on high school and college rifle teams. I would go into school early and train. Then I would train again before going home. The weekends were for matches or all-day training. This should not come as any surprise to you; all Olympians train hard. What I have learned since then is that I did not need to spend that much time and effort.

You see, I did not have a Mental Management System then. If I had, I could have done better on half the effort and half the time. But I am getting ahead of the story.

I vividly remember my first Olympiad in Munich, Germany. It was 1972, and my teammate, Jack Writer, was the best shooter in the world. He had won all three pre-Olympic World Cups and was the hands-down favorite to win the gold. Jack's only problem was me. I occasionally beat him in training. And the occasion was occurring more and more often the closer we got to Olympic day. I thought I was going to win the gold medal, and Jack would take the silver. Olympic day came. I was physically the best in the world the day of the match, but I had not planned for Olympic pressure.

When the match started, I began to shake. I shot nine after nine. I was so scared that I lost the match in my first ten shots due to a poor mental performance. At that time, I felt like my world had ended. I had failed my country, my family and myself. Ten years of training had not fully prepared me to win the gold. I lacked the mental skills. Jack Writer was the champion that day. I managed to win the silver.

Now don't get me wrong. The silver medal is ten times better than the bronze, and the bronze is ten times better than no medal at all. But to my way of thinking, the silver is the closest thing you can get to the gold medal and still lose. I knew that I had to come back to win in 1976. I also knew that to do that, I needed a new mental game.

In 1972, there were no seminars in mental training like the one I teach today. In fact, the only way to learn how to cope with the mental stress of the Olympics was to question Olympic gold medalists on their mental techniques. That is exactly what I did. Over the next two years I spent an average of five hours a day gathering information on the mental aspect of sport. I interviewed champions, asking questions like: "What do you think about when you are performing?" and "What makes you able to win when others fail?"

Like the pieces of a puzzle, my shooting started to come together. In 1974, I established the U.S. national record at 1179/1200, which stood for more than fourteen years. In the World Shooting Championships in Switzerland, I won eight gold medals for my country.

In many ways, I was a different person. I was confident and in control. I had changed mentally. I had changed my self-image. My habits and attitudes were those of a winner. I had developed a system to control the mental aspects of my performance — a Mental Management System. Winning became a habit. In 1976 in Montreal, Canada, my lifelong dream came true. I won an Olympic gold medal. Then, two years later, I repeated as World Champion in Seoul, Korea.

I began teaching the Mental Management System to athletes shortly after the Olympics. I have given seminars on four continents, and the system has been translated into more than a half-dozen languages. I have as clients the Olympic teams of Japan, Korea, India, Taiwan, Canada, Australia and the United States. I have had the pleasure of presenting the Mental Management System to doctors, attorneys, teachers, accountants, directors of sales, and even the United States Secret Service.

And I will outline how this system works and how you can apply it to your life, business and sports in the following pages.

Chapter 2

Why Winners Win

In my more than twenty-five years in competition, I have been both a participant and a winner. I can tell you it is much more satisfying to win. I think everyone knows that. A fact that is not so widely known is that ninety-five percent of all winning is done by only five percent of the participants.

What makes the five percent different? It's not their size, color, nationality or economic situation. It's not anything they are born with — we are all born with the seeds of greatness within us. It is my observation, after competing against and teaching the world's best, that the only thing that separates the winners from the others is the way they think. Winners are convinced they will finish first. The others hope to finish first.

An example of this difference is the great Olympic shooting champion from England, Malcolm Cooper. We were in Seoul, Korea, in 1978 for the World Shooting Championships. Malcolm was favored to win the world title in the standing position, which surprised no one because he held the world record in that event.

Just before the competition was to begin he said, "I'm going to win today!" It wasn't said in a bragging tone. The man was just convinced he was going to win. Then he discovered that his rifle was damaged, and he had to borrow another shooter's rifle for the match.

Then I heard him say, "Wouldn't it be something special to win this match with a borrowed rifle. I'm going to do it!" And that is exactly what he did, setting the world record in the process! You see, he expected to win. That is the difference. I am not saying that everyone who expects to win will always win.

What I am saying is this: If you do not expect to win, you have no chance of winning.

Another example of a champion who expects to win is archer Darrell Pace. I first met Darrell in 1976 at the Olympics. At five feet ten inches tall and only 115 pounds Darrell looked like anything but an Olympic athlete. Yet at the tender age of nineteen, he was already the world champion and world record-holder in archery.

I spent a lot of time with Darrell in Montreal. We would meet together in the evenings, after our training sessions. I was fascinated by Darrell's bold attitude of confidence. He was convinced that there was absolutely no possibility that he could lose the gold medal. He referred to the gold as "My medal." He would say, "I wonder where they are keeping my medal." "Everyone is after my medal, but they cannot take it from me!" He had already won the gold medal in his mind.

I asked him why he was so certain he would win. Darrell's answer was, "I am more committed to mental training than any of my competitors!"

I kept thinking about Darrell as my event drew near. He had helped to reinforce many of my own attitudes on winning. On the day of my event, as I prepared my equipment to compete, I saw Darrell sitting next to my wife, Helen, in the spectator area. "He has come to watch me win," I thought. The time for talking was over. It was a time for winning. We both won our gold medals that year.

I believe the expectation of winning comes from an internal feeling the champion has concerning his performance. He is in harmony with the idea that his expectation and his performance will be equal. In recent years, I have spent most of my time studying what makes the champions consistent winners. I feel certain that most people do not win because they lack a mental system to control their performance under stress. Once this system is in place, winning is possible.

What is your game? Golf? Archery? Tennis? Football? Soccer? Shooting? Selling? Parenting? Managing? Coaching? Teaching? What percentage of what you do is mental? What percentage is pure physical or technique? I have asked that question to hundreds of Olympic athletes and business persons. They all have answered eighty to ninety percent mental!

Performance is ninety percent mental.

To control performance, especially in high-level competition, you need a system. The program that I use and teach is called the Mental Management System.

Mental Management

The process of maximizing the probability of having a consistent mental performance, under pressure, on demand.

I wanted a system that would work all the time, in competition, under pressure. This is such a system. After you read this book, you will never again have the excuse that you could not win because you were not mentally prepared.

An outstanding performance is powerful! Also, an outstanding performance is easy! Only poor performance is plagued by frustration and extra effort. Think about it. When do you expend the greatest effort — when you are doing well or when you are doing poorly? When you are playing golf well, the ball goes straight down the fairway. You do not have to chase it into the rough. You do not spent time looking for the ball. When you play really well, you are balanced and in harmony with your efforts. When I won the Olympics, the actual performance seemed easy for me because I was balanced in my three mental components: the Conscious Mind, the Subconscious Mind and the Self-Image.

The Mental Management System focuses on integrating these components, developing each to its full potential and keeping a careful balance between them. In their most basic form, these mental components are as follows:

The Conscious Mind

This is the source of your thoughts and mental pictures. The Conscious Mind controls all of the senses: seeing, hearing, smelling, tasting and touching. It is what you picture or think about. It is the images that you hold in your mind.

The Subconscious Mind

This is the source of your skills and power to perform. All great performances are accomplished subconsciously. We develop skill through repetition of conscious thought until it becomes automatically performed by the Subconscious Mind.

The Self-Image

It makes you "act like you." The Self-Image is the total of your habits and your attitudes. Your performance and your Self-Image are always equal.

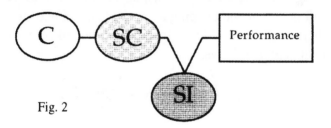

Fig. 2

C Conscious (thoughts)
SC Subconscious (skills)
SI Self-Image (habits and attitudes)

Chapter 3

Principles of Mental Management

Gravity is an irrefutable principle of physics. We all feel the pull of the Earth on us. And just as there are proven principles of physical motion, there are also proven principles of mental success.

The Principles of Mental Management govern how the mind works. These principles are concepts common to winners that have stood the test of time. They work for all people all the time and are applicable to sports performance, business success, and personal development. Remember, success is not an accident. Success follows a set course, and these principles are the boundaries of its path.

PRINCIPLE OF MENTAL MANAGEMENT NUMBER 1

Your mind can only concentrate on one thing at a time. If you are picturing something positive in your mind, it is impossible, at the same

---

time, to picture something negative. And, if you have a negative thought, you cannot, at the same time, think positively.

Why is this principle important? Because it is impossible to picture winning and losing at the same time. You are either picturing something that will help you or something that will hurt you. And, if you constantly control the image in your mind in a positive manner, it is impossible to have a concentration error and a poor performance.

I had a baseball coach once who always said, "Whatever you do Bassham, don't strike out." What do you picture when I say, "Don't strike out." It is impossible to think about hitting the ball if you are picturing striking out. In Olympic-level shooting, I found that it was impossible to concentrate on shooting a ten and count my score at the same time. If my thoughts centered on the score, my performance fell. I had to keep my mental picture centered on performing the shot.

One way to apply a principle is to formulate and use an action statement or affirmation. This statement, written in the first person present tense, describes the action taken when applying the principle.

ACTION STATEMENT FOR PRINCIPLE NUMBER 1:

I take control of what I picture, choosing to think about what I want to create in my life.

PRINCIPLE OF MENTAL MANAGEMENT NUMBER 2

What you say is not important. What you cause yourself or others to picture is crucial.

This is the fundamental principle of successful communication. It is not important what you say, the image your words convey is extremely important. When the coach said, "Whatever you do, Bassham, DON'T STRIKE OUT!", I pictured striking out. He set me up for failure by the way he talked to me. If he had said, "GO STRIKE OUT!", it would have had the same effect on me. Instead, he should have said, "Bassham, HIT THE BALL!"

ACTION STATEMENT FOR PRINCIPLE NUMBER 2:

I always give myself commands in a positive way. I remind myself that what others are picturing, as a result of hearing me speak, is crucial to proper understanding.

When you begin anything — piano lessons or your first day on the golf course — good performance seems difficult. It seems difficult because you are trying to do everything consciously. Most things, such as playing music or sports, require you to do many things at the same time. Because the Conscious Mind can only do one thing at a time, first experiences are very frustrating. The Conscious

Mind needs assistance, which it gets from a second mental process called the Subconscious Mind.

The Subconscious Mind

The Subconscious Mind is where your skills are developed. After that first day of piano lessons, things begin to get easier as you develop skill through practice. Skill is defined as doing something consciously long enough for the process to become automated by the Subconscious Mind.

Unlike the Conscious Mind, the Subconscious can do many things at once. In fact, your brain is like a huge computer. Just how many separate functions can be handled by the Subconscious simultaneously is hard to measure, but we are sure it is in the millions. Yes, your Subconscious Mind can make millions of calculations per second! That is why we need to perform in the Subconscious mode rather than the Conscious. It is vastly more powerful.

A rifle shooter who has Subconscious trigger control will activate the trigger when the sights are aligned. A shooter who Consciously activates the trigger will most probably move the rifle as he shoots, thereby throwing the shot off.

PRINCIPLE OF MENTAL MANAGEMENT NUMBER 3

The Subconscious Mind is the source of all mental power.

This is good news and bad news. The good news is that each of us has within us the power to achieve anything we desire. The bad news is that we are only using five percent of the power available. Why do we use so little? To use more takes both knowledge and effort. Few people know how, and even fewer are willing to put forth the effort. Those who do are consistently among the winners.

Good performance looks easy. One of the most often-watched sports is gymnastics. These fine athletes make their very difficult sport "look" easy. I remember the first time I tried to pull myself up on the rings. That day I gained a great respect for the strength needed to be a gymnast. Their skill comes from years of training. The routines are so well learned that they are Subconsciously automated. My sport of shooting also looks easy, but if you have never done it, the task will be difficult for you.

I once asked a gymnast on the U.S. team what he thought about when he performed. He answered, "I try to feel the flow of the routine. I do not want to think that any element is especially difficult or dangerous while performing."

You perform best when you allow your well-trained Subconscious to do the work. However, the

Conscious Mind can override the Subconscious. When this happens, performance almost always deteriorates. Sleep is a Subconscious action. You may attempt to override the Subconscious by consciously attempting to make yourself GO TO SLEEP NOW. You will probably be up most of the night.

Conscious override is a major problem for athletes on Olympic day. Instead of trusting the Subconscious Mind to perform, athletes try extra hard to do well. Conscious override is the result. You tighten up. You slow down. Off your rhythm, your performance drops. You must allow the Subconscious to do the work. Trust in your ability. Let it flow.

ACTION STATEMENT FOR PRINCIPLE NUMBER 3:

I am so well-trained that all of my performance is Subconsciously done. I trust my Subconscious to guide my performance in competition.

PRINCIPLE OF MENTAL MANAGEMENT NUMBER 4

The Subconscious moves you to do whatever the Conscious Mind is picturing.

When my daughter was nine years old, I asked her to carry a cup of coffee to a guest in our house. Then I said, "Don't spill it!" That was a bad thing to tell her. When she spilled the coffee, I should not have been surprised. After all, I put the idea in her mind. It was my error, not hers. You see, when you say, "Don't spill the coffee!", what picture is created in the Conscious Mind? I picture spilling the coffee. The Subconscious moves you to do whatever the Conscious Mind is picturing, and it is picturing spilling the coffee.

It is the same in sports. There are only four seconds left in the game, time for only one more play. A touchdown is needed to win. The coach calls for his best fullback to carry the ball. He explains the play. "Now young man, you are our only hope to win this game. I want you to go in there and take the hand-off from the quarterback and run in for the touchdown. You can do it!"

In goes the fullback, who explains the play to the quarterback. The quarterback says, "That's great. We are going to win as long as you don't fumble!"

Being positive is our only hope. Positive pictures demand positive results from the Subconscious. If we think negatively, we have to expect negative results.

ACTION STATEMENT FOR PRINCIPLE NUMBER 4:

I realize that my Subconscious power is moving me to perform what I am Consciously picturing. I control what I picture and picture only what I want to see happen.

The Self-Image

PRINCIPLE OF MENTAL MANAGEMENT NUMBER 5

Self-Image and performance are always equal. To change your performance, you must first change your Self-Image.

The mind is like a submarine. The Conscious Mind is the periscope. The Subconscious is the engine, and the Self-Image is the throttle of that engine. The Subconscious is always asking the Conscious Mind what it sees. Then it launches the boat in that direction. The speed is determined by the Self-Image.

The Self-Image, made up of your habits and attitudes, makes you "act like you."

Your Self-Image directs your behavior. This means every person has a special way of behaving. Some people like to get up early in the morning. Some people like to get up late. Some people think they are good in math. Some people are terrified by speaking before a group. Some people hope they can win. Some people expect to win.

We all have our own way of behaving. The sad thing is that most people believe there is nothing they can do about their behavior. They believe that they are the way they are and cannot change. In fact, we are all changing all the time. We experience change as we age. The direction of that change can either be determined by you or for you. If you do not take control of your life, others most surely will. I believe that one of the most important factors in success at the Olympic level is that winning Olympians control their Self-Image growth.

Your Self-Image is like the throttle of the submarine. It controls the speed and distance you can go. We all limit ourselves by our Self-Image. For example, it is not like me to drive my car one-hundred miles an hour. In fact, if I get just a few miles over the speed limit, my Self-Image makes me feel uncomfortable until I slow down. It's not like me to drive fast, so I do not.

Another example is the car salesman who averages selling four cars a month. If he goes the first three weeks without selling a car, his Self-Image makes him work harder to sell four the last week of the month. Also, if he sells four the first week, his Self-Image will slow him down the rest of the month. It is just not like him to sell sixteen cars a month.

We all have a comfort zone, the upper and lower limits being defined by our Self-Image. It is "like us" to operate within this zone. As long as we are in the zone, our Self-Image is content to leave us alone. If, however, we start scoring lower than our limit, the Self-Image will provide us with extra power to improve until we are back within the zone. Likewise, if we start scoring better than our comfort zone, the Self-Image tends to slow us down until we are, once again, back in the zone. Change the zone and we will change the performance. To change the comfort zone, we must change the Self-Image. This relates directly to the sixth Principle of Mental Management.

ACTION STATEMENT FOR PRINCIPLE NUMBER 5:
I am aware that my performance and Self-Image are equal. I am eager to change my habits and attitudes to increase my performance.

PRINCIPLE OF MENTAL MANAGEMENT NUMBER 6
You can replace the Self-Image you have with the Self-Image you want, thereby permanently changing performance!

You can replace the income you have with the income you want.

You can replace the score you have with the score you want.

You can replace the *you* you have with the *you* you want.

The problem for most of us is that we know something has to change for our lives to improve; but we want the change to be in other people or other things, and not in ourselves.

NOTHING IS GOING TO CHANGE UNLESS YOU CHANGE YOURSELF FIRST.

Change is a difficult challenge to face. Most of us think we are pretty good the way we are, and we resist change. Besides, it is easier for us to place the burden to change on someone else, then it's no longer our problem. It takes effort to change.

The Self-Image resists change. Sometimes the Self-Image can talk to you. When your alarm clock sounds early in the morning, you hear, "You're tired. Don't get up! Let's stay in bed all day, then we don't have to worry about working today!" Your Self-Image is the part of your inner self that talks to you. It tells you things like, "What makes you think you are going to win? You've never won before." Or, "We are going to do whatever it takes to win this time!"

ACTION STATEMENT FOR PRINCIPLE NUMBER 6:

I am responsible for changing my Self-Image. I choose the habits and attitudes I want and cause my Self-Image to change accordingly.

PRINCIPLE OF MENTAL MANAGEMENT NUMBER 7

The Principle of Balance: When the Conscious, Subconscious, and Self-Image are all balanced and working together, good performance is easy.

When the Conscious, Subconscious, and Self-Image are balanced and working together, you are in a Triad State. In this state, you work smoothly, efficiently, and seemingly effortlessly toward your goal. It's a wonderful feeling and has been experienced by almost everyone at one time or another. The problem is that we do not experience it often enough.

The key is to experience it under pressure, on demand. Therein lies the challenge. Some can score well in practice, but not in competition. We desire to have that consistent mental performance all the time. That is the definition of Mental Management — the process of improving the probability of having a consistent mental performance, under pressure, on demand.

Chapter 4

The Balance Of Power

In the Triad State, a person is balanced and in harmony, and great performances can become a reality. It is this balance that produces power.

If a baseball player is in the Triad State, he is concentrating on getting a hit, has trained so well that he is swinging Subconsciously, and has the mental attitude that it is "like me" to hit the ball. The result is a hit.

If a salesman is in the Triad State, he is concentrating on solving his client's problem through the sale of his product, has practiced his presentation enough so that it is Subconsciously done. He has the attitude that it is "like me" to make the sale. The result is an order.

One can demonstrate the Triad State by the use of the model in Figure 4.1.

In this model, all the mental processes are equal in size, and the Triad State effect occurs. Good performance seems easy. Perhaps you have experienced this feeling. It's as if nothing can go wrong. When you are balanced, you love your sport and or business activity and have a minimum of challenges. You perform well and it seems effortless.

Fig. 4.1

In fact, you cannot be beaten when you are in the Triad State, unless you face an opponent who is also in the Triad State, and who has superior ability.

However, we are often out of balance, as Figure 4.2 shows. This is a common situation when beginning any new activity: a new job, business, musical instrument or sport. We are out of balance; we have too much Conscious process involved. Though we have good Conscious focus on the activity,

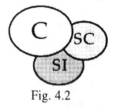

Fig. 4.2

we have not yet developed Subconscious skill. Also, our Self-Image tells us that we are "beginners" and cannot perform well. In this situation, the new activity seems difficult. Remember that first day in piano lessons? If we practice properly and we are encouraged, our Subconscious and Self-Image circles will grow to match the Conscious circle and we will be in balance.

Oftentimes, however, something like the situation in Figure 4.3 occurs. This is an example of

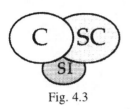

Fig. 4.3

a person who had trained for many years and has acquired exceptional skill, but for whatever reason, his Self-Image has not grown sufficiently. Someone who scores well in training but scores much lower in competition meets this description. This person has all the qualifications to become a success, but as yet does not believe in himself. To perform well, this person must improve his Self-Image circle.

Unfortunately, many people in this situation do not recognize that they must work on their Self-Image. They work instead on their Subconscious skill, becoming even more out of balance.

Figure 4.4 shows the balance of a person who is well-trained and has a good Self-Image, but who is not concentrating on his activity. He is like the "gunslinger" of the old West, who would blow into his barrel after each shot. Then one day he aimed to blow and shot instead.

Fig. 4.4

It is essential always to keep the Conscious Mind on the activity at hand or errors will result. This person must develop better concentration skills or a stronger goal so that the Conscious circle will be in balance with the others.

Figure 4.5 illustrates the problem of overconfidence — a trait the champion must avoid if he is to

stay on top for very long. An over-
confident person has an oversize
Self-Image for the level of
Subconscious skill he possesses.
He always boasts that he will win,
but he falls short because of a lack
of proper preparation. He feels that

Fig. 4.5

he will win because he is wonderful, not because he
is prepared.

There is nothing wrong with having a big Self-
Image as long as you are willing to balance it with
an equally large level of Conscious and
Subconscious skill.

The key point is to learn how to make your
circles larger and keep them in balance. If you have
balanced growth, you have an automatic performance increase without stress and frustration. That
is everyone's aim. We all know that to become better
requires effort and time. What we least want is to
spend a lot of time and energy and not progress.

Every time I notice a frustrated athlete, I
wonder which process is out of balance. If you just
cannot seem to move ahead in your sport or
business, ask yourself these questions:

Am I out of balance?
Am I concentrating on my goals?
Do I really possess the skills to do my job
well?
Do I need more training?

Is it like me to do this job, or do I need to change something about me to do the work?

We are all out of balance at one time or another in our lives. To get back in the Triad State, we must grow the sizes of our process circles. In our next section we will study principles, tools and techniques to increase each of these circles.

ACTION STATEMENT FOR PRINCIPLE NUMBER 7:

I cause my Conscious, Subconscious and Self-Image to move toward being in balance, thereby increasing my performance without frustration.

Section II

Building The
Conscious Circle

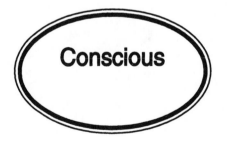

Chapter 5

The Mental Management Goal-Setting System

One habit separates the top five percent of competitors who win from the other ninety-five percent who just play: setting goals. Most people never set them. No surprise there. This is common knowledge.

However, every major corporation sets goals. Every government sets goals. Every builder who builds has a blueprint. Every banker has a written contract on how the borrower is going to pay back each loan. But among individuals, only the super successful ever bother to set personal goals and plan their work.

Some years ago, one of my sons asked me if I would buy him a Ferrari for his high-school graduation present. He knew my answer as he asked the question. I took the opportunity to show him how to set goals by asking him some important questions.

"Son, exactly what is your goal?"

"I want you to buy me a new red Ferrari sports car with brown leather seats."

"When do you want it?"

"Graduation day."

"Why should I do that?"

"It would make your son very happy."

"What do you suppose would be the obstacles to my getting you that car?"

"$125,000 more than you had planned to spend on me."

I said, "So, the only way I have of obtaining that amount of cash is to sell our home or something that valuable. Can you think of any other way?"

"No, Sir."

"Son, do you think the joy I would receive in getting you that car is worth my doing that?"

"No, Dad!"

"You are a smart young man!"

"Thanks, could I have a drum set instead?"

Are our goals just pipe dreams? Are our goals set too high or not high enough? There is a process I have learned from my Olympic training experience that you can use to set your goals just right. I call it the Mental Management Goal-Setting System.

STEP NUMBER 1
Decide exactly what you want.

Find goals that excite you. You must be specific. The more you can identify exactly what you want, the better your chances of obtaining them.

STEP NUMBER 2
Decide when you want it.

Putting a time limit on your goals helps you to formulate a plan to achieve them. If your goal was to save $1,000 in ten years, you could do that by putting about a quarter a day in the bank. If you change the time limit to $1,000 in one month, the plan would have to change.

STEP NUMBER 3
List the pay-value.

Why do you want the goal? List all the reasons that are important to you for achieving the goal. The first rule here is to make certain that the goal you set is big enough to be exciting for you. If it is not exciting, you will not do anything to change your habits or attitudes. It will just not be worth it.

Also, the goal must be your goal, not the goal of another. Is the pay-value personally rewarding to you? I had a friend in college, a pre-dentistry major, who did not want to be a dentist. His grandfather and father were dentists, and the family expected him to join the profession. He hated school as a result.

If the pay-value is not personal, you will not act on your plan. A few years ago, my wife told me she needed new bedroom furniture. She knew exactly what she wanted. Helen provided me with the specific brand, style and number of pieces she desired.

"Helen, this is expensive stuff," I said. "Where am I supposed to get the money to pay for it?"

She replied, "You'll think of something!"

Several weeks passed, and I had completely forgotten about the furniture. I didn't want new bedroom furniture. Helen did. It didn't bother me that the drawers stuck, the finish was scratched and the mirror had a small crack in it. I just kept the light out in the bedroom. When Helen asked how the project was coming along, I said, "I'm working on it."

The next weekend I returned from doing a seminar out of town, and Helen picked me up from the airport. She presented me with several bright new $20 bills.

"Helen, where did you get this money?"

"Remember what you tell your students: To get what you want, you have to get rid of what you don't want. So I sold our bedroom furniture."

Suddenly, I had pay-value invested in new bedroom furniture. My mattress was on the floor and my underwear was in cardboard boxes. Helen's goal became my goal. I had to get that new furniture. But I didn't have the money.

That weekend I attended a shotgun match. I overheard a conversation concerning furniture and guns. I met a man who traded new furniture for used guns. In fifteen minutes, a deal was negotiated. I would receive new bedroom furniture in exchange for a mental management seminar and my shotgun.

STEP NUMBER 4
Determine the obstacles in your way.

Again, you must be specific! What must you do to reach your goals? What habits and attitudes must you change to reach your goal? Remember, nothing is going to get better until you get better. You must change! What must you change? How much additional time must you invest?

STEP NUMBER 5
What is your plan to get your goal?

The difference between a wish and a goal is that a goal has a written plan. Wishes usually do not come true. Goals with written plans are almost always reached. In Step Number 4, you identified several reasons why you were unable to meet your goal. Prepare a written plan to overcome each obstacle. Now the price you must pay for the goal is clear.

Step Number 6
Ask some important questions.

First. Do I really believe my plan will work?

Second. Do I really believe I can work the plan?

Finally. Is the Prize worth the Price?

This is the most important step in the goal-setting process. Ask yourself, "Is the pay-value worth the price I have to pay for it? If the answer is positive, chances are your goal and plan are correct. If the plan and pay-value do not match, you must change something. Maybe you need to change the goal, the time limit or the plan.

Step Number 7
Schedule your plan.

One thing we often fail to remember is that scheduling is a vital part of the planning process. Put your plans on a calendar. I use both a large monthly calendar on my office wall and a day planner I carry with me. If the goal is not scheduled, it will not get done.

When my daughter was eight years old, she overheard me saying, "If it is on the calendar it will get done." The next day I saw marked on my calendar in crayon the words, "Buy Heather a stuffed animal." What do you think I did?

STEP NUMBER 8
Start now.

You are now ready to go. Begin right away. Do not hesitate. Execute the first step of your plan now. Put out high-quality effort, consistently over time, and you can do anything.

STEP NUMBER 9
Never reach a goal without first setting another one.

The day I received my Olympic gold medal was both wonderful and traumatic for me. The award ceremony was great. Hearing my country's national anthem being played while the flag was raised high in front of me was the best of feelings! However, later that day, I had an unexpected experience. I suffered severe depression, and I didn't know why. Helen recognized the problem and helped me understand that I had lost my goal. I had not goal-set beyond the Olympic Games, and I was momentarily without direction. Once I set a new goal, I was again at peace.

STEP NUMBER 10
Never, never quit.

In 1979, I set a goal to win the national title in the air rifle event. I thought that it would take a 380 out of 400 to win. In the match I was down nineteen points with three shots left to go. I shot a nine. Now I had to shoot two tens, I figured, to win. I shot another nine. I was down below 380. I rationalized that I could not win, so I mentally gave up. I quickly put up the rifle and shot an eight. I finished with a 377. That year the national championship went for a 378. Had I been persistent, I would have won the title. Stay with your plan until it is finished.

Chapter 6

The Principle Of Reinforcement

Concentration is nothing more than the control of one's mental picture. Remember, the Subconscious, with all its power, moves you to do whatever the Conscious Mind is picturing. If you can control the picture, you can control the performance. Our Conscious picture is formed from what you think about, talk about, and write about.

PRINCIPLE OF MENTAL MANAGEMENT NUMBER 8
The Principle of Reinforcement. The more we think about, talk about, and write about something happening, we improve the probability of that thing happening!

This is my favorite principle of Mental Management. Every time we think about something happening, we improve the probability that it will happen. Be careful what you think about.What do you picture?

Every time you worry, you improve the probability that what you are worrying about will happen. If you are worrying about scoring badly on an exam, the Subconscious, with all its power, will move you to score badly. It is not what you want, but it is what you will get if you continue to think this way. What you must do is picture scoring well.

Also, be careful what you talk about. I've seen the following situation hundreds of times. Two shooters meet after a match. Shooter A asks, "How did you shoot?" B says, "I did terrible. I shot three nines in a row. Two were out the left for wind and the other one came because I held too long." Shooter B has just improved the probability of having nines the same way in the future because he is thinking and talking about his mistakes.

The really sad thing is that because Shooter A is listening, he is also improving the chance that he will have B's problems in the future. Be careful who you listen to. Do not spend time listening to the problems of others, or you will soon inherit their problems.

I remember presenting a seminar to Olympic shooters. I was asked, "Mr. Bassham, in the 1978 World Championships, you shot a 598/600 to win a medal. What happened on those two nines?" I answered, "Do you really want to know? Do you want to know how I got nines? That will not help you. You don't want to know how I got two nines. What you should be asking is how I got fifty-eight tens. Besides, I can't remember how I got the nines. I do not reinforce bad shots by remembering them."

What you want to talk about is your good shots. By doing that you improve the probability that you will have more good shots in the future.

Be sure to write down what you want. For several years, I have had the pleasure of teaching the Canadian Olympic Shooting Team. In one of the seminars, I remember telling the shooters that it has always been my habit to write down my goals as if they had already been accomplished. At the break, one of the female pistol shooters and I were visiting about her goal to become the 1984 Olympic pistol champion. I suggested that she write down daily, "I am the 1984 Olympic pistol champion!" Only two things could happen, either she would attain her goal or she would stop writing down the goal.

In the Olympics in 1984, this shooter, Linda Thom, tied for the gold medal with another friend of mine, the U.S.A. National Champion, Ruby Fox. In the shoot-off, Linda was victorious, winning the gold medal. Later, we met and talked about her victory. She told me that she knew she was going to win the shoot-off because she had never missed a day writing her goal in her diary. Writing your goal improves the probability that it will be attained.

Be careful not to complain. I often hear people, in business as well as sport, complaining about their circumstances. Complaining is negative reinforcement. I teach my students not to reinforce a bad shot by getting angry. Do not reinforce a bad day at the office by complaining to your spouse. Remember something that you did well each day instead. Fill your thoughts only with your best performances and you cannot help but be successful!

Positive Prediction: Reinforcement in Advance

People perform as we expect them to perform. There is a technique that I call Positive Prediction that is useful in increasing performance. It is a compliment given in advance of a future action. My father once told me that to obtain what you want, you must first provide someone else what they want. Here are some examples:

I receive exceptional service at my local bank. Although I am certain the employees at my bank attempt to provide fine service to everyone, I am positive that I receive special treatment. Why? I use the positive prediction technique. From the very first day I opened my account, I have consistently complimented everyone in the bank, in advance, for their excellent treatment of my business. In return, I have received exceptional treatment. I said to the teller, "I appreciate you. You always have a smile for me when I come in the bank, and you're really good at your job." The tellers have told me they rarely receive this kind of treatment from bank customers, and they look forward to my coming to the bank. I seldom have to stand in a long line. When I come into the bank someone says, "Mr. Bassham, I'll open this station for you." Prediction is an attitude that says, "I expect exceptional service because you are an exceptional person."

Prediction can be harmful if used incorrectly. Eunchul Lee, the World and Olympic Shooting Champion from Korea, was a student at my International Shooting School. Several years ago, after training at my school, Eunchul was shooting with the Korean team in a competition in Mexico City. The Korean coach told me that he did not like Eunchul's prone position. He also informed me that Eunchul's attitude was poor.

I had worked with Eunchul for over a year. This coach had only met him the week before. This coach wanted to win so badly that he had the Korean shooters wound tight as a drum. Eunchul is, by nature, a very friendly and outgoing young man. His coach took this to indicate that he was not serious about his shooting. I told the Korean coach that I respected his ability and that I would look into his criticisms of my shooter as soon as we returned to the U.S.A.

It was fortunate that Eunchul had finished his match before the coach's prediction about his poor attitude and incorrect prone position could influence the match. Eunchul Lee won most of the medals for Korea, including a gold in prone. Later, the Korean coach came to me, apologized, and asked me to look at the prone positions of his other shooters.

When positive prediction is implemented, everyone wins. You feel great using the technique. The person you are talking to gets a lift, and the results make everyone feel wonderful.

Praise: Reinforcement After the Fact

Praise good performance, and the good performance will repeat. If praising others becomes your habit, you will soon become surrounded by competent people who love to work with you.

The teachers in our local school are exceptionally considerate of my children. I called the school office to set an appointment with each of my child's teachers. When I met them they asked, "Mr. Bassham, why did you wish to see me? Is there a problem?"

"No," I replied. "I just wanted to meet you and say that you are one of the most considerate teachers in the school. I am delighted that my child has the opportunity to be in your class. I expect, now that we have met, you will not hesitate to give me a call if there is anything that we can do to aid our child in school."

Teachers are not used to hearing good news. It really makes their day when a parent calls in to compliment rather than complain. How much better would you do your job if you were praised more often?

Praise is an attitude that says, "I recognize exceptional service because you are an exceptional person."

ACTION STATEMENT FOR PRINCIPLE NUMBER 8:

"I choose to think about, talk about and write about what I wish to have happen in my life."

Chapter 7

Rehearsal: The Most Versatile Mental Tool

Though there are a number of mental tools you need in order to win, one of the easiest to understand is rehearsal.

A mental tool is a technique you can use to improve your mental performance. A good mental tool will work all the time, for everyone, at least to some degree. The most often-used mental tool is rehearsal. It has many other names, such as mental imagery and visualization. I prefer the term rehearsal because it is easy to understand. If you have ever been in a play or a show, you know what rehearsal means: practicing for the real thing.

In mental rehearsal you are picturing what you want to see happen before you actually perform. You go over in your mind exactly how you want your performance to be conducted. In rifle shooting, you picture holding the rifle, looking through the sights, centering the target, and firing the shot in the ten ring. The more vivid the picture, the better the outcome. The more often you rehearse, the better the chance for success.

Benefits Of Mental Rehearsal

Rehearsal is mental practice. For the rifle or pistol shooter, it has great advantages. First, you are mentally duplicating everything you do when you are on the range — without going there. You do not have to buy bullets, targets, or wear out your equipment. You do not have to clean up the range or clean your rifle when you finish. And it's cheap! It costs absolutely nothing! And you can do it any time. Also, you rehearse only good performances, so there is no negative reinforcement. Mental practice is a bargain, and done correctly, it is powerfully effective.

You can imagine far more than you currently can achieve. If you consistently rehearse what you want to achieve, what you imagine can become reality. Let me give you an example:

Back in the 1970s, I was shooting good kneeling scores and began approaching the national record of 396/400. I wanted to set the record at 400, a perfect score. But I had never actually fired a 400, even in training.

Nonetheless, I vividly rehearsed shooting the first 100, then another and another. I visualized that last ten shots. Ten. Ten. Ten. Ten. Ten. Only five more to go. Ten. Ten. Ten. Then I rehearsed what I knew would happen at the point: I would realize that I was above the record. Next, I rehearsed hearing a voice say, "That's OK, I do this all the time." Then I imagined shooting two more tens easily and saying to myself, "Another 400, that's like me!"

I rehearsed this sequence several times a day for two months. In my first competition since beginning the rehearsal, I started with a 100 kneeling. My next two targets were also 100s. I began my last series with ten, ten, ten, ten, ten. Only five more to go. Ten. Ten. Ten. Then reality set in. I was above the record. I heard a voice say, "That's OK, I do this all the time." I shot two additional tens, setting the national record at a perfect 400.

PRINCIPLE OF MENTAL MANAGEMENT NUMBER 9

The Self-Image cannot tell the difference between what actually happens and what is vividly imagined.

The imagination is an extremely powerful part of your mind. By rehearsing a 400 kneeling, I convinced my Self-Image that it was like me to shoot a 400 kneeling.

When it is impossible to get to a range, you can also use rehearsal to simulate training. While in the Army from 1976 to 1978, I was assigned to a non-shooting position at Ft. Sam Houston, Texas. I was 250 miles away from an international shooting range. During those two years, I was able to shoot on a range only six days. I also did not attend competitions, except the U.S. nationals and international team tryouts.

Though I could not actually go to the range, I did continue training. I simulated shooting in my spare bedroom, a technique called dry firing, and I rehearsed mentally each day. Result: I made the U.S. international team in 1978 and won the World Championships that year in Seoul.

Mental practice alone cannot replace good range training, but it serves as an effective supplement when actual training is not possible because of weather, injury or time limitations.

Rehearsal Controls Pressure

What is pressure? Pressure is the stress you experience when you are in competition, whether in daily life or sport. If you have to make a critical presentation, speak before a group or perform at the range, you have to deal with pressure. Is pressure good or bad? At first look, it might appear that pressure is always a bad thing. But, I have found in my study of Olympians, that pressure is necessary for top performance. In fact, pressure is neither good nor bad. It is like air and water. Too much or too little and bad consequences occur. Just the right amount of pressure, however, and world records fall.

Pressure can be divided into two parts: Anxiety and Arousal.

Anxiety is fear. We fear many things. We fear serious injury. We fear the unknown. We fear the consequences of having a poor performance. We fear high places, closed-in places, and people and things we do not understand. Fear is not always a bad thing. For instance, fear keeps us from driving our automobiles too fast.

What many people don't understand is that fear can be controlled. One of the best ways to control fear is through experience. You will find that after you have been in a stressful situation often, the negative characteristics of fear will be reduced. Rehearsal can help by giving us mental experience in a pressure situation. I competed in the Olympic Games twice physically, but thousands of times mentally. Rehearsal reduces fear.

The second part of pressure is arousal. Arousal is your level of excitement. If you are just awakening from a deep sleep, you are not aroused enough to have your best performance. You are too relaxed. In contrast, if you have just been told that you have won ten million dollars in the state lottery, you will be too aroused to perform well. There is a point in between relaxation and arousal where your mental performance is maximized. On one side you are too excited, and on the other too relaxed. In the center, between the two, is the optimum mental level, where your best performance can be achieved.

The Arousal Curve

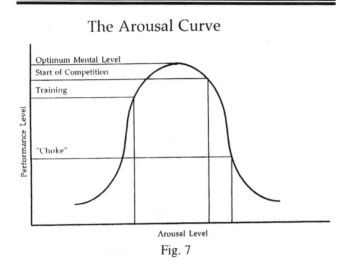

Fig. 7

It is sometimes difficult to attain this optimum mental level. In training, you may be on the relaxed side of the arousal curve. Rehearsing that you are shooting well in a match will move your arousal toward the optimum mental level. In competition, you may be on the excited side of the curve. Again, rehearsing that you are shooting exceptionally well should relax you, moving you toward your optimum level. Rehearsal works well to help you reach this optimum mental level.

Rehearsing your desired performance a few minutes before you begin a match will help center your concentration and move you toward your optimum mental level. I have seen world-class high jumpers rehearse their exact steps just before the jump. In fact, almost all world-class athletes do some form of rehearsal before they perform. Top business executives often use this tool to think through their next move to maximize their efficiency and improve profitability.

Contingency Planning

When NASA trains a space shuttle crew, more than half of the training, I am told, deals with what to do in case of contingencies. In the Olympics or any other shooting match, you must perform well on a particular day. You do not get another chance for a week, a month, or when you are chasing a gold medal, four years. That creates pressure, which affected me negatively in 1972.

But in the 1976 Olympics, I was very calm. One reason: I had rehearsed over and over every possible thing that could happen in the match and how I would respond appropriately. I was confident that I had planned for every possible contingency, which reduced my stress level, allowing me to shoot better.

Rehearsal Restores Relaxation

In 1976, during the final competitions leading up to the Olympics, I had the pleasure of working with Eva Funes, one of America's finest shotgun shooters. Eva's husband, David, related to me that she was unable to sleep the night before major competitions. Poorly rested, she was unable to shoot well the next day. If she took sleeping pills, her reflexes were impaired. David asked if I knew of a mental management technique that would help her.

I told Eva that as long as she was going to be awake all night anyway, she might as well do something productive with her time. I told her to relax in bed and rehearse that she was shooting well in the match. When Eva began to rehearse shooting well, her level of arousal dropped, allowing her to sleep. The next day, Eva Funes, rested from a good night's sleep, won the competition.

Using Rehearsal to Improve Performance

Mary is taking her final exam tomorrow in college algebra. She is frantic, knowing that a poor grade on the final will result in failure for the semester. Recalling a previous history of poor math finals in high school, Mary says, "I've got no chance to pass that test!" With that attitude, Mary has little chance of passing her class.

But Mary need not fail algebra. Mary should rehearse that she is in the classroom, taking the exam. The answers are coming easily to her. She passes the exam and the course.

Rehearsal is no iron-clad guarantee, but it can improve greatly your chances of success. You may effectively use rehearsal to help you get through a negotiation, a law suit, or an income tax audit.

Used properly to reinforce good habits and a winning attitude, rehearsal can greatly improve your chances of shooting success. Rehearsal is the most often-used mental tool because it is logical, easy to use, convenient, inexpensive, and most important, because it works.

Chapter 8

The Three Phases Of
A Task

To properly implement the Mental Management System, you need to understand that everything we do has three parts, or phases:
1. The Anticipation Phase,
2. The Action Phase,
3. The Reinforcement Phase.

The anticipation phase is what you think about immediately before you perform. Running a mental program (see the next chapter) is the anticipation phase of shooting a shot or hitting a golf ball. By running a mental program, you ensure that each shot will be performed exactly the same way.

The action phase is what you think about as you perform. When I shoot a shot, I think about follow-through. I simply continue the hold until the bullet is well out of the barrel. The golfer also thinks about his follow-through as he hits the ball to ensure a good shot.

The reinforcement phase is what you think about immediately after you perform (see Chapter Six). If the shot has been successful, I say, "That's like me!" If the shot is not good, I forget the shot and move directly to the anticipation phase of the next shot.

The difference between the champion and the average shooter or player lies in the edge the champion gains in the anticipation, action and reinforcement phases of performance. Champions carefully prepare for their tasks, concentrate properly while performing, and reinforce all good results.

It's important to understand what these phases mean to Mental Management so that you'll understand how certain techniques I mention later work for you.

The Anticipation Phase

In 1972, as we were packing to journey to Munich, Germany, for the Olympics, my teammate, Jack Writer, approached me with an idea. Both of us were taking two rifles to the games, a primary and a back-up. Jack suggested that I put his back-up rifle in the gun box with my primary rifle, and he would put my back-up rifle in the box with his primary rifle. His idea was that if something happened to one box, we could both shoot in the Olympics. When we arrived at the range in Munich, my gun box was missing. It was recovered, in the locker of the Soviet weight-lifting team, just one day before the competition began. Because of Writer's idea, I was able to train at the Games with my back-up rifle.

The bottom line is that success is no accident. Paying proper attention during the anticipation phase can make your goals easier to accomplish.

The Action Phase

During the 1974 World Shooting Championships in Switzerland, I learned a valuable lesson concerning the action phase. I was a Texas boy, stationed in south Georgia. I had trained that year in temperatures between 50 and 100 degrees. We had the final tryout and national championships at Phoenix, Arizona in June. I won the tryout in temperatures above 100 degrees.

When the world competition began, snow was falling. The temperature was four degrees, and I was bone-chilling cold. I had never shot in snow in my life. I was shooting the 300-meter event. The snow was falling so hard I could not see the target. I was certain they would postpone the match.

Then I heard the range command, "Commence Firing!" The match started. I still could not see the target. I was frustrated. Just then I heard the shooter next to me shoot. I couldn't believe it. What was he shooting at? As I looked downrange I saw that, for an instant, the snow parted, and the targets became visible. The Swiss shooters are experienced in shooting under these conditions. I had no time, nor the opportunity, to become an experienced snow shooter. If I were going to win, I had to shoot as if I had lived in the mountains all my life. So I said to myself, "I am the best snow shooter on this range! I shoot in the snow all the time! I love shooting in the snow!" I watched the Swiss shooter next to me. Every time he readied to shoot, I would follow his lead. I won the match.

Sometimes when your best is not good enough, you have to do whatever is required to win.

The Reinforcement Phase

I have discovered in my twenty years as a teacher that most world-class athletes do well in the anticipation and action phases. However, they often break down in the reinforcement phase. I see far too many athletes reinforcing their bad performances by thinking and talking about them. Every time you talk about a bad performance, you improve the probability of having another one just like it in the future.

I was very fortunate. During the years I competed for the United States, the best shooters in the world were Americans. To win, I had to defeat my teammates.

Jack Writer (World and Olympic Champion), Lones Wigger (World and Olympic Champion), and Margaret Murdock (World and Olympic Silver

Medalist), were seasoned competitors. One thing I especially remember about training with them was that they never talked about their failures in front of me. If Wigger had a problem, he kept it to himself. I asked him about that once. He said he didn't want to give any of us an edge. He once told me, "Bassham, you will likely beat me four out of five times that we shoot against each other, but I plan to make my one time count." He was the toughest shooter in big competitions I ever faced.

Jack Writer was a talker. It was not that Jack bragged on himself, although I can understand how those who didn't know him would think that. Jack just liked to talk. His favorite subject was shooting, and he was his favorite shooter. No matter how many low scores he shot, Jack would only talk about the high ones. The important lesson here is that Writer never reinforced a bad performance and rarely shot a low score in a big match.

Margaret Murdoch rarely talked at all. If she did, it was to compliment others on their performance. I wonder if she knew that every time she praised another shooter, she also improved her own chances of winning?

All three of these champions excelled in the reinforcement phase, each in their own unique manner.

To prepare yourself for competition, you need to ask yourself, how well prepared are you for your task? Are you performing below your potential because you are not properly prepared? Truthfully answering these questions will help your anticipation phase preparation.

Then, ask yourself how well you perform when the circumstances are different from those you have anticipated? This gives you insight into your action phase preparation.

Finally, ask yourself what do you reinforce? Do you praise others when they perform well? Do you praise yourself? If you can answer yes to these questions, pat yourself on the back and continue reinforcing your successes. If not, it's time to start.

Chapter 9

Improving Concentration By Running A Mental Program

To become the best rifle shooter in the world, all I had to do was to learn two things:

Number 1: Perform well enough mentally and technically to score a ten.
Number 2: Repeat Number 1.

Winning requires you to develop a consistent mental picture. The best way I have found to achieve this kind of concentration is by running a mental program.

The mind is very much like a computer. If you input a series of thoughts or commands, you can run a mental program. Most mental inconsistency occurs when the thought process varies from event to event. If you do not have the same picture in the Conscious Mind each time, you should not expect to duplicate the necessary Subconscious skill.

It is possible to duplicate the exact mental series of pictures before every performance, thereby achieving mental consistency. Though I will explain the use of this mental tool by using the examples of shooting a ten and hitting a golf shot, it is easily applied to any activity.

Running a mental program accomplishes two crucial functions:

- The mental program is a series of thoughts, that, when pictured, will trigger the Subconscious to perform the appropriate action.
- The mental program controls the thought process occupying the Conscious Mind. An occupied Conscious Mind cannot pressure out, choke, or have a break in concentration.

The mental program should be run every time for every shot. The program I use and teach has five steps:

1. The Point of Initiation
2. The Point of Attitude
3. The Point of Direction
4. The Point of Control
5. The Point of Focus

The Point Of Initiation

This is the starting point of the program. In rifle shooting, the point of initiation is loading the rifle. Prior to loading, the shooter can think about almost anything as long as it is not negative. However, counting your score before you are finished is always considered an error. The point of initiation may vary from person to person. Some may choose picking up the rifle as the start point. Others may start the mental program after spotting the shot. It does not matter as long as the point of initiation is consistent.

The Point of Attitude

Once the rifle is loaded, the shooter pictures what it feels like to shoot a ten. Picture the feeling of success. See the bullet hole in the center of the ten ring. How does it feel to perform at your best? As you experience this feeling, your Subconscious moves you to get the ten.

The Point of Direction

Next, shift your concentration to what it looks like to get the ten. In this step, you rehearse getting a ten. You imagine proper sight alignment. You imagine the rifle fires. You have a proper follow-through, and a ten is the result.

The Point of Control

In this step, you center concentration on the most critical part of your action. In rifle shooting the point of control is to make the hold slow and small. Think slower, smaller, slower, smaller.

The Point of Focus

The point of focus is the last thing you picture before you fire the rifle and end the mental program. My point of focus is centering the target in the front sight.

The following is a mental program for a golf shot.

POINT OF INITIATION

Grip the club properly. You could also start with assuming the stance or even the club selection. It does not matter as long as it is consistent shot to shot.

POINT OF ATTITUDE

What does it feel like to hit the ball correctly? Decide how you want to play the shot.

POINT OF DIRECTION

Picture a smooth swing, solid contact with the ball, head in the proper position, and good follow-through.

POINT OF CONTROL

Maintain balance and bring the club back straight.

POINT OF FOCUS

Focus on the ball, keeping the head down.

It is necessary to coordinate the mental activity of running the mental program with the physical activity of executing the shot. This takes some practice, but will come in time. Also, you should take care to run the program in training as well as in competition.

By running the mental program, you do not have time to think about anything negative. It is impossible to choke and run the program at the same time. You have to think about choking to choke. If you only run the program, there is no time to think about distractions. You do not have time to count your score. You cannot be distracted by other players. You are protected from failure. It is your insurance policy against a bad performance.

Section III

Building The
Subconscious Circle

Chapter 10

The Skills Factory

I don't think I have a natural ability for shooting. In fact, I am still searching for my special talent. But I have known athletes who seem to have a gift for their sport. One such shooter is Soma Dutta from India.

I met Soma for the first time in 1982. Her family, eager to find an international shooting coach, accompanied her to my International Shooting School in Seguin, Texas, to check me out. Soma stayed at the International Shooting School for one month as we evaluated each other. At the young age of 14, this resident of Calcutta held every major national record in her country. Her records for women and juniors exceeded the best results recorded by the men as well.

Gifted is the only word I know to describe this incredible young athlete. Just as a great artist seems to see the paintings in the mind before they are translated to canvas, Soma had a special feel for her positions. Most shooters tire of training after four to five hours. If I would have allowed it, she would have spent ten. I would insist she take a day off, and then find her sneaking up to the range to shoot.

Soma returned to the school the next year for two months. She shot in the Olympics in 1984 at the age of sixteen, the youngest shooter on the line. She was ranked second in Asia and among the top twenty in the world. She won a coveted quota slot, awarded to fewer than forty shooters in the world, qualifying her to compete in the 1988 Olympic Games in Seoul.

The advantage the gifted athlete possesses is difficult to measure. Obviously, it is not necessary to be especially talented to win the Olympics. I am proof of that. Certain things come easier to the talented ones; for the rest of us, hard work is the great equalizer. Though it is difficult to compare myself to Soma, I believe she masters shooting techniques three to five times faster than I did. The big advantage of talent is that it saves time. If you are not particularly talented, take heart — it may take you a little longer, but you can catch and surpass a talented athlete if you train effectively.

The Subconscious Mind is where your skills are developed and where your training should be focused. The amount of skill and the size of the Subconscious circle is determined by three factors:

1. How often you train,
2. How efficiently you train, and
3. What you reinforce.

To best understand training, we will look at the six guidelines to building Subconscious skills.

TRAINING GUIDELINE NUMBER 1
Catch yourself doing something right.

All too often, I hear the comment, "What am I doing wrong? If I could only isolate my problem areas and find the cause of my failures, I could be a success."

Nothing could be further from the truth. That is like saying if you study all the wrong ways of doing a math problem, you will learn how to do it right. What you really need to do is study the right way of doing things. Isn't it easier to study one way to do something right than a hundred ways to do it wrong? If you study failure, you will become an expert in how to fail.

Therefore, stop catching yourself doing things wrong and trying to find out why you are failing. Instead, only think about your successes, never your failures. An example is the golfer. The mentally uninformed golfer hits a good shot and says, "Well, I guess I just got lucky that time." When he hits a bad shot he says, "Why do I always do that?" The mentally informed golfer hits a bad shot. He knows it is bad, but says, "Next time I will hit a better shot."

Then he hits a good shot and says, "That's a good shot. What did I do right?" See the difference?

TRAINING GUIDELINE NUMBER 2
Train four or five days a week.

The best athletes in the world do not train every day, but you cannot become the best in the world if you do not train regularly. The question to answer is: how much is too much and how much is not enough?

For most activities, business and sport, you will burn out if you do them seven days a week. And if you train less than four days a week, you will not maximize your chance to win.

If you train only one day a week, it is probable that you will deteriorate faster than if you do not train at all. That's right, one day a week is worse than no training at all. If you train two or three days a week, you can maintain your level, but you will not improve. Therefore, train four or five days a week, and work four or five days a week.

TRAINING GUIDELINE NUMBER 3
Wherever you are, be all there.

When you go from the office to the tennis court, leave the office thoughts in the office. When you go home to the family, leave the bad tennis loss on the court. When you go from the home to office, leave the home problems at home. Wherever you are, be there 100 percent.

TRAINING GUIDELINE NUMBER 4
Rehearse the match day within the training session.

Treat every training day as if it had the same importance as the most crucial competition day. You can do that by rehearsing in your mind that each day is the competition. Try to imagine in every practice session that it is the match. See it, hear it, taste it, smell it and feel the match. Make your rehearsal vivid.

TRAINING GUIDELINE NUMBER 5
When you are shooting well, shoot a lot.

This is an expression I borrowed from my teammate in the Olympics, John Writer. It applies to your field of interest as well. I remember one day Jack and I were training together. I asked him what he was going to shoot that day.

"I will shoot 50 shots in the standing position and 100 shots in kneeling," he said.

"I will do the same thing," I said.

We both started shooting standing. Soon I finished my 50 shots and started kneeling. Jack continued in standing. After I finished my 100 shots kneeling, Jack was still in standing. I went to lunch.

When I returned, Jack was still shooting standing. Finally he finished. I asked him why he changed his mind and shot so much standing. That's when he told me, "I was shooting above my record. When I do that I always keep shooting. When you are shooting well, shoot a lot."

The best time to make an appointment is just after you have made a sale. You've heard the expression, "I'm on a roll!" It is really true. When you are performing well, that is the best time to train. Likewise, if you are slicing badly, now is not the time to hit another bucket of balls. If you are having a bad day, stop training. Do not practice losing.

TRAINING GUIDELINE NUMBER 6
We raise or lower ourselves to the standard we are around.

Train with people who are better than you, and you will get better. Always train with people who are not in your league, and soon you will play just like them.

As much as anything else, I owe my success in shooting to having the opportunity to know and train with Lones Wigger, John Writer, Jack Foster and Margaret Murdock. I feel I owe my successes in business to the opportunity of listening to many great businessmen on tape and meeting them in person. Men such as corporate president Rich De Vos have had an important influence on my life. I feel it is vital to be around the winners. Multi-millionaire H. Ross Perot once said, "Eagles never flock, you have to find them one at a time!" The most valuable time in the world is when you can share a few moments with a champion. Do it often enough and you will become the champion. One of the best pieces of advice I have ever received came from a business tape. The speaker, a financial success in his own business, suggested, "Take an expert to lunch." I have learned much from lunch conversations over the years. Many people are reluctant to ask time of the experts and therefore never take advantage of their knowledge. However, an invitation to lunch can change your way of viewing the world.

Seek opportunities to be around people who are where you want to be.

Training Guideline Number 7
Make a bet with yourself, when you win it — pay off!

Set a training objective that requires a special effort on your part. Several examples are:

"When I two-putt three greens in a row, I am buying myself a dozen of those expensive golf balls!"

"When I shoot a 100 kneeling, I am treating myself to a movie!"

"When I reach a weekly business goal, I'm taking my family out to our favorite restaurant!"

Make the bet with yourself that you will attain the goal. When you reach the goal, reward yourself. The reward does not have to be expensive, but it should be something that pleases you and that you can share with others. You will soon find you are working much harder in training and enjoying your improvement.

Follow these guidelines, and you will train efficiently and effectively, and your Subconscious skill circle will grow.

Chapter 11

Performance Analysis

We know from the Mental Management Principle of Reinforcement that we should write down everything that we do correctly. How is this done?

For many years I fought the concept of keeping a performance journal or diary. I worked hard in training, and I wanted to eliminate any superfluous activities. Still, it was not until I discovered a productive journal-keeping system that my training and match scores improved and were much more consistent. With a journal, I was able to review my progress and better evaluate my efforts using a systematic approach to record keeping. The system I use is called performance analysis.

Performance analysis is the process of recording in your performance journal essential information that tracks your progress. It is a complete system, taking only a few minutes a day, that utilizes positive reinforcement to speed you toward your goal.

Why use a performance journal? A plan is not easily followed if it is not written down. It is of no use if you cannot readily refer to it. Your journal should be in a binder that allows you to add and remove pages. Carry it with you to all training sessions. There is a page for each day, with sufficient space to enter the needed data. The purpose of the journal is to add organization to your training program, not burden you with unnecessary work.

A journal contains a written record of six key planning areas.

1. Your schedule
2. Your diary
3. Your solution analysis
4. Your success analysis
5. Your daily goal statement
6. Your index of often-used addresses and phone numbers

Schedule

Your schedule identifies time slots that you plan to devote to some area of your training.

Diary

The next section is called the diary. Fill out the date, location, event (training or competition) and the time of day and duration of the activity. Next, write down exactly what you accomplished during this period. How many shots did you shoot? How many hours did you train? How did you spend the time? If you do not train that day or do anything that affects your sport or activity, do not fill out a journal page.

Three ladies are at a swimming pool. One sits in the sun, never entering the water. The second puts her feet in the water, but does not leave the pool side. The third swims twenty laps in the pool. Later, all three will say they had been swimming that day. It is easy for us to say we are training, when in fact we are spending most of our time visiting with other competitors, setting up equipment, or reflecting upon our condition, whatever it may be.

A journal diary entry eliminates rationalizations and records the facts.

Solution Analysis

Solution analysis is your chance to write down any solutions to challenges you have discovered during a training day. If you have a problem that you cannot find a solution for, simply state, "I'm looking for a solution to ...," and then describe the problem. Also you should write down anything you learned today in this section. Continued reference to this portion of the performance analysis will reduce the chance that you will repeat an error.

Success Analysis

In the success analysis section, write down anything you did well during a day of training. When you do this, you improve the probability that you will repeat the success. If you set a personal record, this section should be quite descriptive on that day. The journal forces you to be positive about your sport and your performance.

Goal Statement

The goal statement is the most important step of the journal page. State an objective that you intend to reach. Write it in the first person present tense, as if you have already reached it. Some examples of goal statements are:

- I often shoot above 390/400.
- I am on the United States Olympic development team.
- I shoot par golf.
- I am the most valuable player on our team.

Goal statements should be achievements that are currently out of reach, but not out of sight. Every time we write down a goal we are that much closer to its attainment. Only two things are possible. Your goal will be reached, or you will stop writing it down. As long as you continue to write down your goal statements, you are moving toward their attainment.

Contacts

Keep these addresses and phone numbers in your address pages:

- Participants in your sport, coaches, administrators, organizers.
- Manufacturers and marketers of products you use in your sport.
- Hotels, motels, and restaurants near competitions you frequent.

Performance analysis is one of the most useful coaching tools. I learn much from reviewing a student's journal. I discover how many days a week the student is training. I know how many hours a day is spent in practice and exactly what was accomplished. I am immediately aware of the student's strengths or problem areas. I know the goals of my students and most important, so do they.

A performance journal provides the athlete and coach with a valuable resource for improvement, without burdening either with unnecessary paperwork.

Be careful to safeguard your journal. I lost my Olympic journal sometime in late 1976. I recommend that you remove the journal pages monthly, storing them in a safe place.

Guidelines for Building a Training Program

Another use for the journal is to document your training program. I will use shooting as the example, but again, the guidelines are easily translated to any sport or business activity.

Begin by determining the competition schedule for the year. In most sports, there are several big meets scheduled for the year, culminating in the nationals. Schedule these events on your master calendar in your journal.

Next, count the number of training days you have available to you until the next competition. Now, count the days available for the entire year. You may be surprised just how few there are.

Look for possible conflicts with your attendance at these special events. College students may not be able to move their finals to go to a match, but they might be able to register for classes that allow them to have Fridays free as travel days. Try to maximize the hours you have available by planning in advance. Too many times, valuable training is lost because we run out of supplies, such as targets or ammunition.

Next, you should file a training budget. If you are fortunate, you have a coach or manager who can help you with this step. A training budget has projections for at least four areas: equipment, travel, fees and supplies.

- What new equipment will you need to reach your goals for the year? What is your plan to acquire them and when is the best time to make purchases?
- What are the travel costs to get to matches, seminars or training sessions? By planning in advance, you may be able to save on advance purchases for air fare or combine two competitions into one trip.
- What fees will be charged for entering competitions, national association memberships, seminars and coaching.
- What supplies will you use; include ammunition, targets and cleaning supplies. Avoid the possibility of lost training days by scheduling advance purchases of these essential items.

You divide your year into quarterly sessions. The length of the quarters are individual and sport-specific.

During the first quarter of a training year, after you have just finished a needed rest from last season's competitions, evaluate your performance. During this session, you should ·establish your training plan, make out your budget and set your schedule for the year. Evaluate any equipment or technique changes you plan to make in the coming competitive year. Now is the time to test new ideas. Order new equipment, evaluate it, and make improvements during this session. Later in the competition phase, you will not want to change things.

During the second quarter, concentrate on conditioning. In this quarter, you work especially hard on drills that will strengthen you for the demanding season ahead. Shooting is not a seasonal sport. We shoot major competitions year round. If your sport is not seasonal, you may have to compete within the conditioning session. If so, understand that your competition has the same challenge. It was always motivating to me to shoot against my major competitors in the winter season. If I seemed behind, I worked harder. If I was ahead, I worked even harder because I knew that the competition would be trying to catch me.

During the third quarter, you are ready for competition. During this period, you will be attending major competitions leading up to your national championship. By this time, you should be properly conditioned and at your best. The focus in this session is peak performance. Training centers on match simulations rather than drills. Avoid experimentation with new equipment and techniques.

During the fourth quarter, rest and reflect on how the season progressed. You have done your best in the nationals. It is a time for much needed rest, repair and reflection. Do not make the mistake of omitting this step. You may think that you can get a jump on your competition by training at this time, but chances are you will instead weaken yourself in the long run. Also, you need the time away from your sport to reflect on your goals, training methods and concepts. It is during this period that you establish an outline for your training during the year.

Finally, you should set up training objectives for the year in three major areas. First, determine what objectives you want to meet in training by the end of each quarter session. Second, determine how many hours you will average in each training day. Third, plan how you will spend those hours. By following these guidelines, you can develop a well-planned training program that should improve your results in competition.

Section IV

Building The Self-Image Circle

Chapter 12

Building A Better You

The Self-Image is the sum of your habits and attitudes. Your attitudes determine whether you feel positively or negatively about an item or concept. Your habits determine how you act. You will do certain things because it is consistent with your Self-Image.

Are these attitudes familiar?

- I perform great in practice, but when I get in the match, my score drops.
- If I do well at the beginning, I lose it at the end.
- I am so busy, but I just don't seem to get much done.
- I can never remember names.
- I can't sell anything. I'm not that kind of person.

- I could never speak before a large crowd of people.
- I'm technically sound in my sport, but I choke under pressure.

These are statements I've heard from students of mine. They are all temporary Self-Image attitudes. They can change. In fact, the same people who held these attitudes initially soon began to talk like this:

- I perform better in matches than in practice.
- If I start well, I finish well.
- I am an efficient person who gets things done.
- I'm good at remembering names.
- I enjoy speaking before groups.
- I'm the kind of person who people order from.
- I can count on a good performance, especially under pressure.

What accounted for the change? They all experienced a change in Self-Image. When you shift the Self-Image, the change is permanent.

We tend to perform within a certain "comfort zone." I bowl between 120 and 160. It is not like me to bowl below 120 or above 160. It is like me to bowl an occasional strike, but I have never bowled four in a row. I get nervous when I bowl three in a row. It is not like me to hit four strikes in a row. I'm comfortable between 120 and 160. That's like me.

Your Self-Image "makes you act like you." It keeps you within your comfort zone. If you are below your zone, your Self-Image makes you uncomfortable and turns up your power until you are within the zone. Likewise, if you are above your zone, the Self-Image will cut your power, dropping you back within your zone. As long as you "act like you," the Self-Image is content and does not interfere. To change your performance you must change your Self-Image and elevate your comfort zone.

Changing your Self-Image is the most important skill you will ever learn. You can change any attitude you do not like. When the Self-Image changes, performance changes. To change Self-Image, one must accomplish four very important tasks:

1. You must be willing to undergo change.
2. You must identify the habits and attitudes that you need to change.
3. You must set up a new Self-Image that is in direct conflict with your old self.
4. You must exchange your old Self-Image for the desired new Self-Image.

You Must Be Willing To Change

Nothing is going to change unless you change. If you possessed everything that you needed to succeed, you would have reached your goal already.

As an example, Donny was a fine young basketball player who had a chance to make his school's starting squad. His defensive ability was solid. He was a good shooter, but his percentage at the free-throw line was poor. So poor in fact that the coach hesitated to play him in critical situations. The coach knew that Donny's deficiency was a mental attitude about the free-throw line. When questioned about his not starting, Donny would say, "The coach just likes the other player better. I just don't shoot free-throws well. I never have." With that attitude Donny had no chance to start. Also, Donny has a bad habit of getting mad when he misses a free-throw, thereby reinforcing his error. Donny needed to change his Self-Image. His attitude needed to be, "I am the best free-throw shooter on the team."

One day Donny approached the coach.

"OK, coach, I'm ready to do whatever it takes to make the starting squad. What do I have to do?"

"Are you ready to change your attitude about making free-throws?"

"Yes, coach, I'm ready!"

Identify The Attitudes And Habits You Need To Change

How do you identify which habits and attitudes you need to change? It is easier than you think. Simply look at the problems you are having and start there. If you turn your weaknesses into strengths, your performance will surely benefit. In this regard, problems and frustrations are valuable keys to your success. For skilled athletes and business professionals, most of the time their problems are negative attitudes and poor reinforcement.

In our example, Donny needs to change one attitude and one habit. The attitude that needs changing is his opinion of himself: "I am not a good free-throw shooter." Also, he must eliminate reinforcing his missed shots.

Set Up A New Self-Image That Is In Direct Conflict With Your Old Habits And Attitudes

Donny's new attitude is, "I am the best free-throw shooter on my team." His new habit is, that each time he makes a free-throw he must say, "That's like me!" Each time he misses, he must forget his error. Olympic athletes call this technique Feast or Forget.

He must run a mental program on each free-throw to maximize his chance of making every shot. He should reinforce his successes by recording his performance analysis in his journal.

Exchange Your Old Self-Image For The Desired New One

Replacing an old Self-Image with a new one is no simple matter. Our habits and attitudes were instilled over a long period of time and are not easily dislodged. You must be careful undergoing any process that can so alter your behavior. The mental process that I endorse is both safe and extremely effective. It has been carefully evaluated by the coaches and professional staffs of the Olympic teams of a half dozen nations. It is called the Directive Affirmation, and I cover its use in the next chapter.

Chapter 13

The Directive Affirmation: The Most Powerful Tool For Changing The Self-Image

Developed in its present form shortly before the 1976 Olympics, I personally credit the Directive Affirmation with having the greatest single effect on my success in athletics and business. Once you have mastered this Mental Management tool, you can change anything you do not like about yourself. You can use the Directive Affirmation to help you achieve anything you desire in your life. This concept is not magic, but it certainly seems to work like it. I used this tool to win the 1976 Olympics and the World Championships in 1978.

The Directive Affirmation is effective for increasing productivity, reducing the negative effects of stress and creating winning attitudes.

The Directive Affirmation is a paragraph written in the first person present tense that describes a person's goal, pay-value of the goal, plan to reach a goal and habits and attitudes affecting the goal. It is rehearsed repetitively, causing the Self-Image to change.

To illustrate how the tool works, we will use the example of Donny the basketball player.

Writing A Directive Affirmation

Step 1: Define the goal. In Donny's case, it was to become the best free-throw shooter on his team. He would write it as, "I am the best free-throw shooter on my team."

Step 2: Set a time limit. Donny would run the Directive Affirmation for 21 days from the start date.

Step 3: List the personal pay-value of reaching this goal. Donny would write, "I will be a starter on the basketball team. I will help my team win because I score well at the free-throw line."

Step 4: Outline the plan to achieve the goal.

A. Run a Mental Program before each free-throw in practice and in games.

B. Every time I score I will say, "That's like me!"

C. Record my performance analysis daily.

D. Read and visualize my Directive Affirmations daily.

Step 5: Write a Directive Affirmation in the first person present tense, beginning with the word I. State the goal as if you already are in possession of it. Next list the pay-value. List your plan to reach your goal. Restate the goal. Date the paragraph with your target date.

Donny's Directive Affirmation might be:

> *11/1/95. I am the best free-throw shooter on my team. I start each game and enjoy the chance to help my team win by making free-throws. I always run a mental program before each shot and reinforce each successful basket by saying, "That's Like Me!" Also, I record my performance analysis and read and visualize my Directive Affirmation daily. I am the best free-throw shooter on my team.*

Step 6: Make five copies of the Directive Affirmation in your own handwriting on five-by-seven file cards.

Step 7: Place the cards in five prominent places, such as your bathroom mirror, on the refrigerator door, on your desk, on your computer terminal, on the bedroom door, as a bookmark in the book you are reading. These places are called key points.

Step 8: Read and visualize your Directive Affirmation each time you come to a key point. A key point is a suitable location for a Directive Affirmation card. It should be a place that you visit often in your normal day. Each time Donny comes to a key point, he must read and visualize the Directive Affirmation. See yourself as the person in the Directive Affirmation. Run the Directive Affirmation for twenty-one days, then remove it and rest for nine days. Then you may modify the previous Directive Affirmation; or, if totally satisfied with the results, replace it; or, if you need more time, repeat the same Directive Affirmation. Soon, as your Self-Image changes, you will become the person described in the Directive Affirmation. Your performance will Subconsciously improve.

When Donny begins to read the Directive Affirmation, he sees himself as being the best free-throw shooter on his team. He pictures starting every game and making a contribution to his team. He sees himself running a mental program, sinking the basket, and saying, "That's Like Me!" Donny records his successes in his performance journal and reads and visualizes his Directive Affirmations daily. Each session should only take a few minutes.

This is not the way Donny has thought of himself in the past. This new Self-Image is in direct conflict with his old Self-Image. The Self-Image cannot stand a conflict. Something has to go; it will be the new Self-Image or the old one. As Donny continues to visualize the "new Donny" in the Directive Affirmation, at some point the conflict is resolved by the exchange of the old attitudes and habits with the new ones. Wham! The Self-Image is changed, and Donny starts sinking free-throws.

Reshaping the mind is much like reshaping the physical body. If you are overweight, it is likely that the cause is repetitive overeating. Repetitive change of your eating habits is the best way to bring your weight down safely. If you have a poor attitude, it is likely that the cause is repetitive negative reinforcement. Repetitive change of your thinking habits is the best way to bring about an attitude change.

The real power in the Directive Affirmation is that it requires the user to set a goal, list a pay-value, set a time limit, identify a plan to get the goal by changing an attitude or habit (or both), and repeat over and over each day a new positive picture.

Does this sound familiar? You know that you should do these things, but unless there is a way to require yourself to do them, you won't! How many times have you read a self-improvement book or attended a seminar, after which you came home all excited, but two weeks later you were the same old person. If any change occurred in you at all, it was temporary.

The Directive Affirmation is a tool to affect permanent change. If you follow the steps in the Directive Affirmation carefully, there are only two possible outcomes. Either you will become the person you want to be or you will stop reading the affirmation. It is that simple.

Chapter 14

Making The Directive Affirmation Work For You

In more than fifteen years experience using and teaching the Directive Affirmation, I have seen phenomenal results in a broad range of applications. In this chapter I will list several examples of Directive Affirmations as applied to various success areas.

Directive Affirmation For Weight Control

People are not successful in dieting because they have their goal stated incorrectly. If you are ten pounds overweight, the goal should not be to lose ten pounds — it should be to lose the weight and keep it off. Instead, you go on your favorite diet. This normally means you alter your eating habits. This is not like you, and your old Self-Image begins to fight you from the very beginning. Still, you persist, and after some time you notice a drop of a few pounds. Since your goal is to lose ten pounds, you continue until you are ten pounds lighter. Then an amazing thing happens. For you to continue to reach your goal of losing weight, you must gain weight again. Soon you are ten pounds heavier again. The cycle then repeats. I know people who have lost a thousand pounds with this method, ten pounds down — and then up — at a time.

A better way is to set the correct goal. If you weigh 170 and want to weigh 160, then set the goal to maintain a fit 160-pound weight.

Let's set up a Directive Affirmation to achieve a desired body weight. Using the Directive Affirmation, you will find that your diet is easier to follow, and you will experience a change in Self-Image. You will not have to lose the weight again.

DIRECTIVE AFFIRMATION:

Step 1:   Define the goal. To weigh 160 pounds.

Step 2:   Set the time limit. Two months from now.

Step 3:   List the personal pay-value of reaching this goal. "I feel better and look better at 160. I can wear my best suit comfortably."

Step 4:   Outline the plan to achieve the goal.

A.   Eat fruit for breakfast.

B.   Drink a food supplement or eat a food bar for lunch.

C. Eat only at mealtimes (no snacks between meals).
D. Ride exercise bike daily for thirty minutes.
E. Read and visualize my Directive Affirmations daily for twenty-one days.

Step 5:   Write a Directive Affirmation.

11/1/96. I weigh 160 pounds. I feel and look great at 160. I enjoy wearing my best suit in comfort. I eat fruit for breakfast, food bar or liquid supplement for lunch and only eat at mealtimes. I ride my exercise bike daily for thirty minutes. I read and visualize my Directive Affirmations daily. I weigh 160 pounds.

Directive Affirmation To Become A Non-Smoker

Many smokers find it difficult to stop smoking and not return to their old Self-Image of being a smoker. Again, the difficulty is due to setting the wrong goal. The goal should not be to stop smoking; it should be to become a non-smoker. If your goal is to stop smoking, to attain your goal, it is necessary to begin smoking again. You stop, then start, then stop, then start again. There is a better way. With the Directive Affirmation, change is permanent.

DIRECTIVE AFFIRMATION:

Step 1: Define the goal. To become a non-smoker.

Step 2: Set the time limit. Twenty-one days from now.

Step 3: List the personal pay-value of reaching this goal: "I have prolonged endurance, more energy and longer life expectancy."

Step 4: Outline the plan to achieve the goal.

A. I permit no cigarettes in my home.

B. I chew gum when I feel like smoking.

C. I say continually, "I control my life, not a chemical."

D. Read and visualize my Directive Affirmations daily.

Step 5: Write a Directive Affirmation.

11/1/96. I enjoy being a non-smoker. I feel strong, healthy, with more energy. I know I will live longer. I permit no cigarettes in my home. I chew gum when needed, and I continually say, "I control my life, not a chemical." I read and visualize my Directive Affirmations daily. I enjoy being a non-smoker.

Directive Affirmation For Making an Olympic Shooting Team

I thought you might like to see the Directive Affirmation I utilized to make the Olympic team in

1976. The same format can be used for any high-level goal for competition.

Directive Affirmation:

Step 1: Define the goal. To become a member of the 1976 U.S. Olympic Shooting Team.

Step 2: Set the time limit. By 1 July 1976.

Step 3: List the personal pay-value of reaching this goal.

A. I have taken my next step toward winning the Olympic Games.

B. I enjoy the recognition of being one of the best shooters in my country.

C. I have qualified for an all-expense-paid trip to Montreal, Canada, to compete for the Olympic gold medal.

Step 4: Outline the plan to achieve the goal.

A. Use ultimate-you actual rehearsal before each stage (Editor's note: an advanced mental rehearsal technique developed by Lanny), run a mental program on each shot, record my performance analysis daily and rehearse winning the gold medal each evening.

B. Train five days a week, five hours a day, using progressive training of dry firing, group shooting and live shooting.

C. Jog three miles four times a week.

D. Supplement my diet with Nutrilite XX daily.

E. Read and visualize my Directive
Affirmations daily.

Step 5: Write a Directive Affirmation.

*7/1/76. I am a member of the 1976
U.S. Olympic Shooting Team. I have taken
my next step toward the accomplishment of
my lifelong goal —an Olympic gold medal.
I enjoy the recognition as one of the best
shooters in my country. I look forward to the
all-expense-paid trip to Montreal to
compete at the Games. I always rehearse
before each shooting session. run a mental
program on each shot. record my performance analysis daily and rehearse winning
the gold medal each evening. I train five
days a week. five hours a day. utilizing
progressive training of dry firing. group
shooting. and live shooting. I jog three
miles. four times a week and eat my
Nutrilite XX food supplement daily. I read
and visualize my Directive Affirmations
daily. I am a member of the 1976 U.S.
Olympic Shooting Team.*

Directive Affirmation For Remembering Names

Occasionally, we need an affirmation to
change something about ourselves that we do not
like. Some of us are poor at remembering names.
This Directive Affirmation should make you good at
remembering names for the rest of your life.

DIRECTIVE AFFIRMATION:

Step 1:   Define the goal. To become good at remembering names.

Step 2:   Set the time limit. One month from today.

Step 3:   List the personal pay-value of reaching this goal.

A. I feel good when I can remember a person's name.

B. They feel good as well.

C. Remembering names is good for business.

Step 4:   Outline the plan to achieve the goal.

The major reason why people cannot remember the names of others is that they have poor name-remembering habits. When most of us meet a new person, we do not even hear their name. We are too busy saying our own name. If you will implement the following habits, you will become gifted in recalling names.

When I meet a new person I:

A. Repeat their name.

B. Spell it.

C. Form an association with their name and a familiar item.

D. Later write it down.

Step 5:   Write a Directive Affirmation.

6/1/96. I am good at remembering names. When I recall a new person's name. it makes me feel good. It also makes them feel good, and it is good for business. When I meet a new person, I always repeat their name, spell it, form an association, and later write it down. I am good at remembering names.

Directive Affirmation For Becoming A Better Time Manager

Time is the only asset you cannot recover once it is lost. Becoming a good time manager should be high on any successful person's list of skills. There are many useful books available on time management. Many people find implementing the suggestions in these books difficult. The Directive Affirmation is just the tool to solve this difficulty.

THE DIRECTIVE AFFIRMATION:

Step 1:   Define the goal. To become a good time manager.

Step 2:   Set the time limit. Twenty-one days out.

Step 3:   List the personal pay-value of reaching this goal.

A. I feel organized.

B. I get many things done in a short time.

C. I can find the information I am looking for easily.

Step 4:   Outline the plan to achieve the goal.

A. I keep all my notes, calendar, addresses,

and schedules in a journal that I always keep with me.

B. I write out a things-to-do list before the beginning of each day, ranking each item and scheduling the most important first.

C. I keep a clear desk and work on only one item at a time.

Step 5:   Write a Directive Affirmation.

8/1/96. I am a good manager of my time. I am well organized, getting things done in an efficient, timely manner. I can find information that I am looking for easily. I keep all my notes, calendar, addresses, and schedules in a journal that I always keep with me. I write out a things-to-do list before the beginning of each day, ranking each item and scheduling the most important first. I keep a clear desk and work on only one item at a time. I am a good manager of my time.

Directive Affirmation To Become Debt-Free

You can even use the Directive Affirmation to help with the bills. We live in a day of credit cards and easy credit. With the inflating costs of homes and autos, it is no wonder that most people must deal with more and more debt. The major reason more people are not debt-free is that they never goal-set to become debt-free. We often goal-set to increase our income, but when the income increases, we simply increase our "needs." The Directive Affirmation can help.

DIRECTIVE AFFIRMATION:

Step 1:   Define the goal. To become debt-free. To owe no one.

Step 2:   Set the time limit. Within two to five years of today's date. Run for twenty-one days, rest nine, repeat if necessary. (Remember, you only have to use the Directive Affirmation until your Self-Image changes. Then, if you continue focusing on the goal, your Subconscious will provide the power to achieve it.)

Step 3:   List the personal pay-value of reaching this goal.

Debt equals stress. Imagine life with no mortgage, no credit card balances, no loans outstanding and no fear of bankruptcy.

Step 4:   Outline the plan to achieve the goal. If the goal is more than one year away, as in this case, focus on a key objective that is along the goal's path. You may have to move through three or four objectives to achieve your long-term goal.

A.   Invest ten percent of all you earn in an interest-bearing program.

B.   Stop all charge card and credit purchases.

C.   Set up a budget to live on less than you earn, apply the balance to reducing debt.

D. Aggressively seek out opportunity to increase your income, applying the increase toward the debt.

Step 5: Write a Directive Affirmation.

> *12/1/2001. I am debt-free. I pay no interest. I have no mortgage, no credit card balances and no loans due. I am financially free. I invest ten percent of everything I earn in an interest-bearing program. I pay cash for what I purchase. I set up a budget to live on less than I earn, applying the difference toward reducing debt. I aggressively seek out opportunities to increase my income, applying a portion of the increase toward the debt. I am debt-free.*

Directive Affirmation For Passing Exams

For students who are concerned about finals, or professionals who are concerned about state boards, this Directive Affirmation will make you a better test-taker.

DIRECTIVE AFFIRMATION:

Step 1: Define the goal. To make an A on the final exam in Mental Management 101.

Step 2: Set the time limit. The exam date.

Step 3: List the personal pay-value of reaching this goal.

A. Passing the exam is necessary for passing the course.

B. I will have taken a vital step toward graduation.

C. I will enjoy the feeling of scoring high on the exam.

Step 4: Outline the plan to achieve the goal.

A. I prepare for the classes by reading the assigned text before class and finishing the homework.

B. I take good notes in class.

C. I study adequately for the final.

D. I rehearse taking the final, knowing the answers, and scoring well.

E. I read and visualize my Directive Affirmation daily.

Step 5: Write a Directive Affirmation.

12/1/96. I made an A on my final exam in Mental Management 101. I enjoy the feeling of making a top grade on this final. I have passed the course and taken a vital step toward graduation from the Thrill of Victory University. I prepared for the final by reading the assigned text, turning in my homework in a timely manner, taking good notes, and studying for the exams. I rehearsed taking the final, knowing the answers, and scoring well. I read and visualize my Directive Affirmation daily. I made an A on my final exam in Mental Management 101. ·

Directive Affirmation For Starting Your Own Business

A Directive Affirmation can be written for any goal, even if you are unsure of a plan to acquire the goal. Here is an example a student of mine used to start his own business.

DIRECTIVE AFFIRMATION:

Step 1:   Define the goal. To start my own business with a higher salary than I presently earn, without having to move from the city.

Step 2:   Set the time limit. Six months from now.

Step 3:   List the personal pay-value of reaching this goal.

A. More money to enhance my lifestyle.

B. Change in job will eliminate burn-out.

C. I will enjoy the feeling of moving upward in my community.

D. I will control my finances.

Step 4:   Outline the plan to achieve the goal.

A. Looking for a way to start a better-paying business.

B. Rehearse beginning a new business with higher pay.

C. Read and visualize my Directive Affirmation daily.

Step 5:   Write a Directive Affirmation.

12/1/96. I enjoy running my new business here in my community. I enjoy the feeling of moving up in my financial position. I am excited about the increased income I am receiving. I created this new business by staying open to any new idea that would increase my income, rehearsing that I founded a higher-paying business in the city, and reading and visualizing my Directive Affirmation daily.

Now write a Directive Affirmation for your goal, using the examples in this chapter. Follow the checks below to ensure you have written the affirmation correctly.

1. Is the goal one you want personally? Is it exciting to you?
2. Did you place the time limit at least twenty-one days and no more than one year from today's date? Goals that are years in the future must be fragmented into objectives that you can work on within the next year.
3. Do your goals set up a conflict between your current Self-Image and the Self-Image you wish to acquire?
4. Did you begin with the word I?
5. Did you write the statements in the first person present or past tense? Be careful not to use future tense such as, "I want to win the national championships," or "I plan to win the championships." Instead, write, "I am the national champion."

6. Did you write a statement describing the pay-value to you for achieving the goal?
7. Did you write a statement detailing how you plan to achieve the goal?
8. Did you repeat the goal statement?

Follow these guidelines, and you will be able to write an effective Directive Affirmation for your goals.

Chapter 15

Become A Promoter

My father often told a story about a cowboy in a bar who was continually bragging to the bartender about the quality of his horse.

"My horse is the best-looking, best-trained, smartest animal in the state!"

"I'd like to buy a horse like that. How much is he?" asked the bartender.

"Not for sale at any price. Everyone says he's the finest horse they have ever seen. I'm just proud to own him."

Finally, the bartender could not stand it any more and offered the cowboy such a high price that a sale was made. The next day the bartender was furious when he came to the bar.

"Where is that cheat who sold me the horse!" the barkeep raved. Then he spotted the cowboy.

"The animal is lame, ugly, untrained, and worthless! You can't ride him. He's cross-eyed and sway-backed. What do you have to say for yourself, cowboy?

"I've just one thing to say," the cowboy drawled. "If you don't quit cutting down that horse, you ain't never gonna sell him."

My favorite word in the English language is "promotion." The cowboy was successful because he was a good promoter. Webster defines promote as "to raise or move forward to a higher or better position, to further the growth of something, or to work actively, stirring up interest in an idea or concept." This is a powerful word.

A good mental manager is a promoter. I suggest three areas that we should promote:

1. Our systems,
2. Ourselves,
3. The Self-Image growth of others.

Promoting Systems

I am not an expert in politics, but I suggest that if we had a society filled with people promoting the country, instead of verbally tearing it down, we could achieve greater things as a nation. We must loudly champion the things that are right about our system, while silently going about changing the things that are wrong. Too many times, it is the other way around.

Athletes must promote their national associations and national governing bodies. We must promote our coaches, team administrators and managers. I spent twenty years as an athlete, ten of those years on the U.S. national team. Within the past eleven years, I have been a coach, teacher, administrator, and a parent of athletes. I have gained a tremendous respect for those supporting sports activities. When I competed, I am certain that I was not always supportive of the people who ran the matches, the organizers or the administrators. I could not fully appreciate the difficulty of their tasks until I had walked in their shoes.

If you are in business, you must praise your profession, your industry, your company and product as well as those you work for and with.

Gold medals are never won alone.

If you are a parent of an athlete, I respect you for sacrificing for your children. I am the father of three. My boys are twins and both are involved in shooting. When I buy equipment, I have to buy two sets of everything.

If you are a coach, I respect you for your diligence. When the team wins, everyone says, "The athletes did it!" When it loses, they say, "It's the fault of the coach!" Most of the coaches I know are volunteers. Their only reward is the occasional praise they receive. They are never paid enough.

Finally, and most important, we must not forget the role played by the wives and husbands of the champions. The cost for an Olympic gold medal is great, especially for the spouse. After winning my gold medal, many people surrounded me at the functions my wife and I attended. One day, I noticed that they had pushed Helen away from me. She was not seen as an important factor in the win. All they wanted was the medalist. I stopped the interview, joined my wife, and held her close.

For the three years prior to my first Olympics, I spent more nights away from my family than I did at home. Helen squeezed every penny out of our budget for extra ammunition. We never went on a vacation, we always took my vacation time at another rifle match. She did not complain. The gold medal is ours, together.

Promoting Ourselves

It has become socially acceptable in our society to present ourselves as being less than acceptable when we speak to others. Recently, I heard a lady compliment another woman, saying, "What a nice dress!" Her friend answered, "What, this old thing!"

You cannot expect people to think well of you if you are not willing to think well of yourself. I am not saying that we should boast. But I have had just about enough of people apologizing for being competent. I can assure you the Olympic champions I know do not hold their heads down when a compliment is offered. Do not be afraid of accepting the sincere praise offered by others. Say "Thank You!"

out loud, and say silently to yourself, "That's like me!" The best way to promote yourself is to control your self-talk. Say, "I am getting better at that!" rather than "I always do that poorly!"

You can promote inner growth by feeding your mind positive information through reading and listening. I encourage you to listen to tape recordings of motivational speakers while you drive your car. Your library is full of books on the subjects of being positive, self-improvement and personal growth. Reading is a wonderful way to inherit the success of the writers. Make your mind a depository of positive information.

Promoting Others

Building Self-Image in others is a primary task of parents, teachers and coaches. I offer six simple suggestions to promote the growth of your students and children.

1. Look them in the eye. When you are speaking or listening to someone, you are building them up when you look right at them. Conversely, you tear them down by looking away. Eye contact shows you are concerned about the other person and that you place a high value on the person you are speaking with.
2. A name is everything. Nicknames can build up or tear down. Ask yourself, is a

name aiding or hindering a student? How does the student feel about the name? If they do not value the name, do not use it.

Many years ago, Helen and I selected what we thought was the most beautiful name we had ever heard for a little girl. That is how our daughter Heather Dawn got her name. When she was little, I called her "Heather-Belle" and Helen called her "Doodle." Now, that she is an adult, "Doodle" just doesn't fit anymore. She will always be my Heather-Belle, I just won't call her that in front of anyone.

3. Praise in public, correct in private. No one is motivated by being chewed-out in front of their peers. I see far too many coaches who break this rule. This practice tears down Self-Image. Public praise builds Self-Image.

4. Praise twice as much as you correct. Remember, you are building by praising. There is no question that corrections must be made in a tactful, timely manner. But you build Self-Image by promoting more often than you criticize.

5. Never steal a dream or limit a goal. My twin sons Brian and Troy were excellent soccer players when they were young. One summer, we saw an advertisement

in the newspaper about a five-week, European/Soviet soccer tour. The team would play in seven countries, including the Soviet Union. Tryouts were to be held in San Antonio, Houston, and Austin to select only sixteen boys from the state of Texas. When Brian, Troy and I arrived at the tryout, we discovered that the participants, once selected, would have to raise over $2,500 each to offset costs. When these facts were announced, over seventy-five percent of the boys walked off the field before try-outs began.

My sons came to me and said, "Dad, do you think we have a chance to make this team? Should we try out?" I replied, "You can't win if you don't enter!" They both made the team. It was a tremendous effort, but both boys raised $2,500 each from contributions made by local merchants and businesses in our little town of Seguin. Their dream was realized.

6. Never give up on anyone. In the late 1950s and early 1960s, the U.S. Army Marksmanship Unit shooters began to dominate international shooting. During this period, one of the shooters stayed on the bench his first three years on the

army team. He was unable to make the U.S. national team. The army questioned his ability; it seemed he just did not have what it took to become a champion.

The shooter resigned from the army, but he returned to active duty within a year to make the 1964 U.S. Olympic Team. That year Lones Wigger Jr. won an Olympic gold medal, setting a new world record. Wigger is the most successful athlete in international competition in the history of this country. He has won more medals, made more U.S. teams, and set more world records than any other American in any sport.

The point: some people choose their own time to become a champion. Do not give the appearance that you have given up on your students or children. Also, giving up on yourself brings down your Self-Image faster than any other factor.

Become a promoter of your organization, of yourself and of others.

Chapter 16

Answers

One of the deficiencies of a book is that you cannot ask the author a question. As I present seminars, I am frequently asked the same questions repeatedly. I thought you might be interested in the answers to some of these questions about the Mental Management System.

What should I do when problems occur?

When challenges occur in your attempt to achieve a goal, you must respond with appropriate and timely solutions. Most people view problems as obstacles that keep them from their goals. Instead, problems and frustrations help them identify the areas of needed growth. In this regard, problems are valuable. Also, they make us appreciate our successes, as the next principle shows:

PRINCIPLE OF MENTAL MANAGEMENT
NUMBER 10

The Principle of Value: We appreciate things in direct proportion to the price we pay for them.

I have noticed in my seminars that when students have their tuition paid by their sport associations, they are attentive, but rarely write anything down. When they pay their own tuition, they take good notes. People appreciate things in direct proportion to the price they pay for them.

People who have to struggle for many years to achieve their goal appreciate success even more. If you are experiencing some challenges in the journey toward your goal, this is not only quite common, but absolutely essential. Finding solutions to problems is essential to growth and provides a sincere appreciation of the accomplishment of the goal.

ACTION STATEMENT FOR PRINCIPLE
NUMBER 10:

I realize that the problems I must overcome to reach my goals, just increase the value of the goals, once they are achieved.

How many Directive Affirmations may I run at once?

The limiting factor in running a Directive Affirmation is the number of good key points you have available. You should not have more than one Directive Affirmation at a key point. If you can find ten key points then you may run two Directive Affirmations at the same time. I have never been able to run more than two at once.

How much time should I spend at a key point?

You should carefully read and visualize your Directive Affirmation at each key point. In the first few days, this procedure may take two to three minutes at each key point. The time will shorten with practice. Soon, your Directive Affirmation will run automatically at anything that resembles your key point. If you have as a key point your refrigerator, you may find that your Directive Affirmation will run as you approach any refrigerator.

When do I stop running the Directive Affirmation?

Run the Directive Affirmation for twenty-one days only, then take at least nine days rest. Your job is not *Consciously* to try to achieve your goal. Your concern is only to run the Directive Affirmation. Soon, your Self-Image will change, and you will notice a corresponding change in your performance.

Were you nervous at the 1976 Olympics?

Yes! I have always gotten nervous in big competitions. I still get nervous before every seminar I present. I am the most nervous when I am watching my children in competition.

It is acceptable to be nervous before your competitions. In fact, I would be worried if my students were not at least a little aroused just before the Olympics. The key point is that it is permissible to be nervous before you perform, as long as you are not nervous as you perform.

By using the Mental Management System, I was not excessively nervous while I was shooting on Olympic day. I reached the optimum mental level before I started shooting through Ultimate You Actual Rehearsal. I ran a mental program on each shot of the match and reinforced each good shot. I was not nervous while I was shooting. I had developed Subconscious skill through a well-designed training program. I had developed the kind of the Self-Image habits and attitudes that were consistent with winning the gold medal. I was in the Triad State. You need never be excessively nervous while you are competing if you properly utilize the Mental Management System.

What did it feel like to win the Olympics?

When I remember the 1976 Olympic games, I recall four separate emotional experiences. Shooting the match was like walking on the edge of a knife blade. I was behind my teammate, Margaret Murdock, for most of the match. We shot 120 shots in the Olympic three-position match, forty in each of the prone, standing and kneeling positions. At the end of the prone stage, Margaret lead me by a few points. Margaret is the best standing shooter under pressure I have ever faced. She turned in a miracle performance standing. I performed well, but I was trailing her by five points going into kneeling.

I knew I had to shoot the best kneeling of my life to win. The weather was horrid. The wind was strong and tricky. I could make no mistakes in this position. I walked that knife edge, turning in the best kneeling of my life. When I had finished, I felt I had won the medal. I was not certain of Margaret's score, but I felt like the gold medalist at that point. I had actually shot a 100 on one of my ten-shot strings. I was especially proud of that. Waiting for the official result was like aging ten years for every hour. International rifle shooting is not like the 100-yard dash, where the winner is immediately known. The scoring of the targets in our match took three hours to complete. The first set of scores to be put up on the results board are unofficial, pending protest. These scores are rarely changed. My score was the last to go up. Unofficially, Margaret had won the match by one point. I had another silver. The reporters had been waiting for three hours. They wanted a champion to interview. They would wait no longer. Margaret Murdock was surrounded by reporters. I was alone.

I knew immediately that something was wrong. I have lost close contests before. I did not, at any time, feel like I had lost this match. I quickly looked up at the scores. They had made an error on my 100 kneeling score. It was scored a 99. That was incorrect. Several people had watched me shoot every shot, including Jack Foster (World Champion in rifle), Darrell Pace, and my wife, Helen. All had scored that string a 100. A protest was called for. Another hour passed before the official and final results were posted.

Verification of a gold-medal performance is always a positive feeling. The score keepers had incorrectly marked one of my tens a nine. I was the Olympic Champion, but just as I had not felt a feeling of loss at the first score, I did not have a feeling of intense joy as the final score was posted. I could not help looking at Margaret. She had allowed herself to believe that she had won the medal. Now, it had been stripped away. We had equal scores, but under International Shooting Union rules, the tie was broken by the highest last ten shots. It was a bad rule. Either duplicate medals should have been awarded, or we should have had a shoot off for the gold. (Editor's note: Lanny petitioned the International Olympic Committee to award duplicate gold medals. They declined.)

Finally, I remember the feeling of sharing. Every athlete in the Olympics yearns for the day when they are standing on the top step of the three-tiered platform while their national anthem is played. As the first notes of the Star Spangled Banner were played, I brought Margaret up on the top tier. We stood together as the anthem was played. It was the only time this has happened in Olympic history. I did not feel complete as the Olympic Champion until Margaret joined me on that platform. As long as I live, that shall remain the most special of feelings.

Chapter 17

Seven Strategies Of The Mentally Tough

People who are successful at having consistent mental performances under pressure seem to do many things alike. Some of these examples come from the world of shooting, some come from the world of business, and some of them from other sports that I've been around and observed over the years.

Number One: The Principle of Transportation

The principle of transportation is a critically important way to shorten the amount of time you need to move from being just good at what you do to being great.

This is what I mean by transportation. Let's say you are performing at a certain level, and you want to evolve to a much higher level. The fastest way to accomplish this is to transport the habits and attitudes you need to perform at the higher level and adopt them today. In essence, you mentally transport yourself to a higher level of performance.

You imagine yourself being in complete command of the skills necessary to succeed at the higher level. For instance, let's say you are a member of a national team, and you want to become a national champion. Mentally take yourself to a national champion position. Now you're national champion. Take a look around. What habits and attitudes would you have if you were the best in the country? How would you feel about other shooters you compete against? Would you be in awe of anyone? No. Examine your attitude about how you would shoot under pressure at the national championships. How would you feel knowing you were the best shooter in the country?

Would your habits and attitudes be different than they are now? Of course. Once you make that transportation to a higher level, and you look around and discover a habit or an attitude that's different than what you have today, grab hold of the champion's habits and attitudes and bring them back to where you are today. Have those attitudes today. Dump the attitudes that you had.

I had to use the principle of transportation to make my first Olympic team. At the Army Marksmanship Unit, everybody there was already world or Olympic champion, and I had to think and act like them in order to beat them. I asked myself, "What if I was beating these people? How would I think about them? What habits and attitudes would I have?" Once I determined the answers to those questions, I started thinking like a champion instead of the way I had been thinking. Instead of looking at Jack Writer or Lones Wigger and being in awe of them, I started thinking that I could beat them.

If you read Tom Watson's book about the building of IBM, you'll learn how that computer company was built. He visualized how he wanted the company to be when it was full-blown and operating at its highest level. And he asked himself, "How would we be acting?" "How would we be treating our customers?" "What kinds of things would we be doing if IBM existed as a big company?" Then he took those answers and applied them to his business in the beginning.

Don't live in the present mentally. Use the principle of transportation to take you where you want to be.

Number Two: Your Past Is Not A Prison

Mentally tough people do not think about the past. The past can be a prison. Your present is not your potential. How you perform today doesn't determine how you will perform in the future — unless you allow your past to become a prison.

Do you recall the story of Dan Jansen, the Olympic speed skater? After three attempts at the gold, Jansen was winless. The 1994 Olympics was certain to be his last chance. The media called him snake-bit. In past attempts, Jansen had always fallen.

You see, speed skating requires risk. To skate fast, one must skate on the edge, risking a fall. Jansen had been entered in two events. His first, the shorter of the two, was his best. The world-record holder in this event, Jansen was favored to win. He went all out, on the edge, but just like all the times before, Jansen slipped and lost the gold.

I recall watching this drama unfold on TV. After the race, Jansen's coach was walking toward the locker room. A reporter asked him, "What's wrong with Dan? Is he just snake-bit? Looked like the ice was slippery!"

I will remember the coach's reply forever, "The ice is always slippery."

Tired and taunted by the media, Dan had one more race to skate. Would Dan risk the edge again or play it safe? Would he listen to the past calling to him? Would it be his prison forever?

On that day Dan Jansen skated on the edge to victory. He finally won his gold medal. He will always be remembered for his courage.

Don't give in to your past. Don't let your past become a prison.

Number Three: Imitate The Champions

Find out what the best people in your sport or business are doing, and duplicate what they do.

Take a good look at what the best people in sport do in training, determine how they look, figure out how they think. Then you train, think and look just like them.

If your way of performing is unique — no one else in the world performs like you — and you're world champion, that's called innovative. But if you look different from everyone else in the world and you're not the world champion, that's called naive. Being different can be innovative or devastating, depending on whether or not you win.

A safer, saner approach is to match the existing standards in the sport by duplicating what the best shooters do. Then, you can increase the standard.

Find out what the top people in the world are thinking, doing, planning and testing. I guarantee you the top one percent in the world are not thinking like the other ninety-nine percent.

If you think and train like most people, you'll perform like most people. If that's OK with you, that's fine. If you don't mind being in the middle of the pack, that's OK. But if you want to break out and win and succeed, you are going to have to think differently than the mainstream does.

How do you find out what the champions are doing? Ask them. Most people don't because they're afraid of bothering them. People wonder if the good performers will talk to them. Well, the good shooters darn well won't talk to you if you don't ask them. You've got to go out of your way to meet the champions. The national championships are a great place to meet the champions. But sometimes you have to be willing to go to the places where these people train.

It is easier than you think to learn how a champion prepares. If you really want to know something, take a champion to dinner. Buy a five dollar hamburger and see if you can get a million dollars worth of information out of that. Most national champions I know are very willing to share their knowledge with other people.

Number Four: Train Hard, Compete Easy

The mentally tough work hard in training, much harder than their competition. Training five or more hours a day five days a week is not uncommon among Olympians. They find more efficient ways to train. They focus on maximizing their equipment advantage, and if there are any technical advances out there, they find them.

It might surprise you to know that I designed the stock on the rifle I used to win the Olympics. I designed about fifty bad stocks before I made a good one. I can't tell you how many pieces of wood I bought. I was looking for an edge, and I knew the stock I built, which I won the World Championships with in 1974, would give me an edge in 1976.

I took it to Dieter Anschütz, owner of the famous Anschütz company, makers of most of the rifles used in the Olympics, and showed him some plans for my stock. Dieter is one of the great men of shooting and a good friend of mine, but he told me, "Lanny, Lanny, Lanny. You are the master shooter. I am the master gun-builder. I won't tell you how to shoot, and you don't tell me how to make guns." That was the end of that discussion.

So, I went to Walther, his major competitor. The Walther rifle had a good trigger and an accurate barreled action, but it also had a pretty poorly designed stock for my style of shooting. I took leave from the Army, bought a plane ticket, flew to Ulm, Germany, and went in to see Mr. Peter Hoffman of Karl Walther GmBh.

At that time, I was a silver medalist, so I got their attention.

Engineers in white coats came in, and I proudly showed them my plans for the stock. I asked them, "Do you think you can make this?" They took some measurements, and then they left. Hoffman told me to go back to my hotel, but that we would have dinner that night, and for me to plan to come back the next day. I asked him, "Do you think they can make that design?" He said he wasn't sure, but we would check tomorrow.

The next day, I returned to the factory, and waiting for me were two complete rifles. Totally finished. They had stayed up all night long making them. The rifles were exact replicas of my plans. I went home with these two rifles, and I used them in 1976 to win the gold medal and in 1978 to win the World Championships. It gave me an edge. Dieter Anschütz has never really gotten over turning me down. That decision surely cost him some sales to Walther.

You don't have to be a stock designer or anything like that to get an edge. But you need to find an edge. The edge I found was not so much the stock design, but the attitude that I was willing to go the extra mile. I was willing to do things my competition wasn't willing to do. Outwork your competition. Be more effective in your profession or sport. Go the extra mile.

Then, when you get in a match, try hard enough to shoot well, but not one percent more. More medals are lost by good shooters trying too hard in a competition than by any other factor.

Nine out of ten of the people that come to me and take the Mental Management Seminars have the common problem of trying too hard in competition. We know where this attitude comes from. We're taught all our lives that the harder we try, the better we'll do in competition. This is not true in competition. You can try too hard and have your score go down.

There's a level of effort expended which gives you the best performance; it is similar to the amount of effort you put out when you have a really good practice day. It's easy to shoot when you're shooting well. Don't over-try in competition. Try just the right amount.

Number Five: Visualize Before Game Day

I don't recommend practicing the day before a competition. But I do recommend that you train mentally.

If it's possible, the day before a competition, go to the point you're assigned to, sit down at the point, and mentally go through the competition. Rehearse your strategies. Rehearse how early you'll get to the line. Where are you going to sit? Where are you going to put your equipment? How will you lay things out? What is your sighter strategy? How do you want the match to flow if everything works perfectly? What are the dominant conditions. What will you look for? Go through some contingency-planning rehearsal.

Then go to the finals area and rehearse shooting well on point eight, seven, six — all of them — since you won't know which one you'll be on. Rehearse what you expect to do. The actual day of competition, your Subconscious will be coded, like a guided missile, with the kind of performance you expect to have.

Success in your business or profession will certainly be enhanced if you rehearse your actions mentally prior to a crucial activity. That's a strategy of people who win.

Number Six: Take All Problems As Positive

You cannot always control what happens in your life; what matters is how you handle what happens.

Everything that happens to you has a positive side, if only you'll look at it. Problems may look negative, they may feel disturbing, but if you look at problems from enough perspectives, you'll find they have a positive side.

For me, thank goodness, I had my terrible mental performance in 1972 and won a silver medal instead of a gold medal. If I hadn't gotten a silver medal, I wouldn't have studied mental management, I wouldn't know any of this material, and I would have missed a wonderful life. Because of my failure in Munich, I have had the wonderful opportunity to teach the best in the world how to be better. I feel so blessed because of that failure.

Do you have a problem and look at it as disaster. Or do you have a problem and look at it as opportunity? Burke Hedges writes in his book, *You Can't Steal Second with Your Foot On First!* that being fired from your dead-end job might be the best thing that could happen to you. Now you are free to entertain options in your life that you could not see being trapped in your job. His suggestion is to start your own business.

Obstacles are only obstacles when you allow them to be. Shut the door on the past and open the door of the future.

Problems tell us when we're going in the wrong direction. Problems identify areas we need to work on. Problems can be helpful, if you're willing to use them to find solutions. If you have a problem, ask yourself, "What can this do for me?"

The best advice on handling problems that I have ever given to Olympians is to ask this question: "Who is the one person in the world who can best help me solve this problem?" Now, forget about your problem until you are in front of the one person that you have chosen to help you. Most important, do not discuss your problem with anyone else on God's green earth. To do that is reinforcing the problem, not finding the solution. That's being mentally tough.

Number Seven: Have Big Dreams

My hope for you is that you don't settle for mediocrity. Don't let the good life keep you from

the great life. I hope you have huge, huge, unbeliev-
able dreams.

Dreams will drive you to accomplish great
things. I wouldn't have sacrificed nearly as much as
I did to have a *good* shooting career. But I was more
than willing to sacrifice what I did to have a *great*
shooting career. It was worth it.

If you have a big dream, you'll be ready to
take on big tasks to achieve it. You'll be willing,
even enthusiastic to prepare for big jobs.

It doesn't have to be an Olympic dream.
Consider financial independence. Few people even
come close. I feel one reason is that they are willing
to settle for an average life. They do what their
friends do and end up where their friends are going.
Where your friends are headed may be fine for you
if they are headed where you want to go, but if they
are not, you might consider dreaming bigger.

I made the decision in 1979 to leave the
military with the rank of major. I enjoyed the service
to my country, but I did not control my life. The
Army did. I had a bigger idea, to own my own
business. I knew that ninety-five percent of the
medals taken in competition were taken by five
percent of the participants. I also knew that ninety-
five percent of the wealth in America was in the
hands of business owners, not those who worked for
them.

I decided to dream bigger and began my own
business. That business today provides substantial

incomes for thousands of families in twelve states in the United States and seven other countries around the world.

There are costs to dreaming big. You'll know you've set a big goal — dreamed a big dream — when the wheels in your life begin to fall off. Some big obstacle will come rolling down on you, showing you that you shouldn't dream that dream. But it's just a test of your mettle. It's a test to see if you're worthy of achieving your goal.

The next thing that will happen when you dream big is that doors of opportunity will open wide. Things happen when you dream big.

The third thing that happens when you set a big goal is that you get energized. You get so excited that you're able to do things that were impossible for you to do before.

Dream big, and big rewards will follow.

Chapter 18

Cease Firing

In the past quarter century, I have observed Olympians from two unique perspectives, as an Olympian myself and as an Olympic Coach. Olympians separate themselves from all other athletes. Olympic medalists separate themselves from all Olympians. Gold medalists separate themselves from all medalists, and Bonnie Blair and Al Oerter separate themselves from all other Gold medalists.

I have observed a pattern of thinking as I have worked with these elite people. In every group or population of people, one finds eighty percent thinking one way, fifteen percent thinking nearly the opposite (the leaders) and the top five percent who innovate. It is the focus of this book to describe the innovations I have observed in the area of Mental Management. My goal is that you might become one of the top five percent in your sport or business.

The time has come to wrap up. I hope you have gained valuable assistance from this book.

If a slow, short, uncoordinated kid can become an Olympic champion, then it must be the mental and not the physical abilities that earn the medals.

Performance is a function of three mental processes: controlling the Conscious Mind, the Subconscious Mind, and the Self-Image.

Mental Management is the process of maximizing the probability of having a consistent mental performance, under pressure, on demand.

Ten Principles of Mental Management:

1. When the Conscious Mind has a positive thought, it cannot, at the same time, be thinking negatively.
2. What you picture is crucial.
3. The Subconscious Mind is the source of all mental power.
4. The Subconscious moves you to do whatever the Conscious Mind is picturing.
5. The Self-Image and performance are always equal.
6. You can replace the Self-Image you have with the Self-Image you want, and, therefore, permanently change performance.

7. When the Conscious, Subconscious, and Self-Image are balanced and working together, good performances are effortless.

8. The more we think about, talk about, or write about something happening, we improve the probability of that thing happening.

9. The Self-Image cannot tell the difference between what actually happens and what is vividly imagined.

10. We value things in direct proportion to the price we pay for them.

The Mental Management Goal-Setting System is used to help determine the correct goal, plan and timetable for anything you desire to achieve. Its steps are as follows:

1. Decide exactly what you want.
2. Decide when you want it.
3. List the pay-value.
4. Determine your obstacles.
5. Determine a plan to get the goal.
6. Ask important questions, including "Is the prize worth the price?"
7. Schedule the plan.
8. Start now.
9. Never reach a goal without first setting another one.
10. Never, never quit.

Rehearsal is the most versatile mental tool and is extremely useful for mental practice, controlling pressure and contingency planning.

A mental program is composed of five points:
1. The Point of Initiation
2. The Point of Attitude
3. The Point of Direction
4. The Point of Control
5. The Point of Focus

Skills are developed by:
• Catching yourself doing something right,
• Training four or five days a week,
• Being all there, wherever you are,
• Rehearsing the match day within training sessions,
• Continuing with the activity when you are performing well,
• Surrounding yourself with those who are superior to yourself.

Performance analysis is the champion's way of keeping a performance journal.

To change the Self-Image, you must:
• Be willing to change,
• Identify the habits and attitudes you need to change,
• Set up a new Self-Image in conflict with the old one,

• Exchange the old Self-Image with the new one.

The most powerful tool in Mental Management is the Directive Affirmation. It has eight steps:

1. Define the goal.
2. Run it for twenty-one days, rest nine days, then repeat if necessary.
3. List the personal pay-value of reaching a goal.
4. Outline the plan to reach the goal.
5. Write a Directive Affirmation.
6. Make five copies on cards.
7. Place the cards in prominent key points.
8. Read and visualize your Directive Affirmations daily.

We must promote our systems, ourselves, and others.

A friend of mine is a fireman. He tells a story about a great apartment fire in the city. The fire spread so fast that the only way the people in the top floor could be saved was to place a ladder from the roof to the window of an adjacent building. The people were forced to crawl across the ladder to safety. The ladder was ten stories above the ground.

Everyone was saved except a woman and her six-year-old son. The woman was afraid of heights, so the fireman, at the risk of his life, crawled across the ladder, rescuing her son. From the window the fireman called to the woman, "Come across now, the fire is close." She would not move. She kept looking down at the street below.

The fireman did the only thing he could have done to save the woman. He took her son back across the ladder. He said, "If your son is to live, you are going to have to save him!"

She did.

It was not like the woman to cross the ladder, but it was like her to save her son.

You are in control of what you Consciously think about, your Subconscious skills and your Self-Image growth. You have a ladder to cross. It is the ladder of performance and it leads to your dreams.

If you are interested in improving your mental performance or the mental perfor- mance of your organization call Mental Management Systems at 800-879-5079.

For more products, information about training,
and to sign up for our free email newsletter,
MENTALCOACH, visit:
www.mentalmanagement.com
Or call: (972) 899 - 9640